Expanding Literacy Practices Across Multiple Modes and Languages for Multilingual Students

A Volume in:
The University of Miami School of Education and Human Development Series

Series Editor

Luciana C. de Oliveira

The University of Miami School of Education and Human Development Series

Series Editor
Luciana C. de Oliveira
University of Miami

Expanding Literacy Practices Across Multiple Modes and Languages for Multilingual Students

Edited by

Luciana C. de Oliveira
Blaine E. Smith

INFORMATION AGE PUBLISHING, INC.
Charlotte, NC • www.infoagepub.com

Library of Congress Cataloging-In-Publication Data

The CIP data for this book can be found on the Library of Congress website (loc.gov).

Paperback 978-1-64113-480-4
Hardcover: 978-1-64113-481-1
eBook: 978-1-64113-482-8

CONTENTS

PREFACE

Luciana C. de Oliveira and Blaine E. Smith

Literacy practices have changed over the past several years to incorporate modes of representation much broader than language alone, in which the textual is also related to the visual, the audio, the spatial, etc. This book focuses on research and instructional practices necessary for integrating an expanded view of literacy in the classroom that offers multiple points of entry for all students. Projects highlighted in this book incorporate multiple modes of communication (e.g., visual, aural, textual) through various digital and print-based written formats. In addition, this book particularly focuses on the possibilities that this expanded view of literacy holds for emergent to advanced bilingual students and scaffolds necessary for supporting them. Our focus is specifically multilingual students as classrooms across the United States and other English-speaking countries around the world become more and more diverse. The book considers educators as active participants in social change and contributors to our overall goal of social justice for all.

This book grew out of work conducted by doctoral students and former doctoral students, now faculty at various universities, from the Language and Literacy Learning in Multilingual Settings (LLLMS) specialization in the Department of Teaching and Learning at the School of Education and Human Development at the University of Miami, Florida. The most outstanding feature of this work is the breadth of examples for integrating literacy in the classroom, as well as the specific instructional strategies provided for supporting multilingual students. This

Expanding Literacy Practices Across Multiple Modes and
Languages for Multilingual Students, pages vii–ix.
Copyright © 2019 by Information Age Publishing

volume is unique in tackling both literacy and specific scaffolding for multilingual students. Additionally, the chapters here collectively aim to go beyond describing research to also provide a variety of classroom connections for practitioners and implications for teacher education.

In Chapter 1, "Teaching Multimodal Practices to Multilingual Elementary Students through Picture Books", Sharon L. Smith examines research surrounding methods for analyzing pictures books from a multimodal perspective and studies that have carried out such analysis. Through a synthesis of current research, this chapter identifies overarching themes across the literature. Situated in the contemporary circumstances in which students are daily bombarded with multimodal texts, this chapter provides teacher educators and practitioners with practical steps to apply theory into practice in their classroom and equip all students with the strategies and tools necessary to carry out multimodal discourse analysis (MDA) on picture books.

Chapter 2, "Exploring Multimodal Representations in a Fourth Grade English Language Arts Teacher Guide to Support Emergent Bilinguals' Vocabulary Instruction", by Irina Malova, Alain Bengochea, Susan R. Massey, and Mary A. Avalos, draws on results of vocabulary instruction and learning activities for emergent bilinguals from a recent content analysis of a fourth-grade English Language Arts teacher's guide. This chapter describes how multimodal texts—texts with different types of media used–visuals, gestures, sounds—are designed to support learning about words during whole-group lessons. The authors provide suggestions for extending the use of multimodal resources and approaches beyond the teacher's guide to support emergent bilinguals' English vocabulary learning using an established framework for multimodal instruction.

In Chapter 3, "Using Multimodal Practices to Support Students' Access to Academic Language and Content in Spanish and English", Sabrina F. Sembiante, J. Andrés Ramírez, and Luciana C. de Oliveira consider the potential for expanding literacy practices to include multimodal literacy for emergent-to-advanced bilingual (EAB) students in dual language programs. They showcase how teachers can apply a multimodal literacy approach in their teaching to support students' access to academic language and content in Spanish and English texts. The chapter discussed purposes of the images and texts in U.S. English and Spanish-language textbooks and the manner in which they can be utilized to develop students' bilingual academic content knowledge and language in the content areas.

Chapter 4, "Collaborative Writing with English Language Learners: A Review of Research and Implications for Practice", by Loren Jones, discusses how collaborative writing can be used as a strategy for writing instruction that teachers can draw on to support the writing development of their students, especially English language learners (ELLs). This chapter synthesizes and interprets the current empirical research on collaborative writing in the elementary context. At a time when educators are searching for ways to effectively support students in becoming proficient writers, this chapter puts forth a framework for teachers to implement collaborative writing in their classrooms.

In Chapter 5, "Translanguaging for Literacy Development at the Elementary Level", Carolina Rossato de Almeida reviews the literature on translanguaging as a writing practice and offer insights on its benefits, suggestions on how to incorporate creative assignments in the classroom, and implications and considerations for teachers. This chapter concludes with some questions that remain regarding the implementation of translanguaging as pedagogy.

In Chapter 6, "Scaffolding Multimodal Composing for the Multilingual Classroom", Blaine E. Smith and Daryl Axelrod describe the key concepts of a multimodal framework and review main benefits of multimodal composing for bi/multilingual students. They provide specific scaffolding strategies for supporting students' multimodal composing process and discuss implications for teacher education.

In Chapter 7, "Writing for Social Justice: A Promising Practice for Culturally and Linguistically Diverse Adolescents", Kristin Kibler reviews the literature on social justice writing projects for culturally and linguistically diverse adolescents and provides recommendations for practitioners. Since social justice education is meant to challenge and counter misconceptions and stereotypes that lead to structural inequality and discrimination, the chapter highlights ways to provide students with resources to reach their full learning potential, build on each student's talents and strengths, and create a learning environment that promotes critical thinking and increases student agency for social change.

CHAPTER 1

TEACHING MULTIMODAL PRACTICES TO MULTILINGUAL ELEMENTARY STUDENTS THROUGH PICTURE BOOKS

Sharon L. Smith

Multimodal analysis of picture books provides a way to examine image-text relationships in children's narratives. This chapter examines research surrounding methods for analyzing pictures books from a multimodal perspective and studies that have carried out through such analysis. Through a synthesis of current research, it identifies overarching themes across the literature. Situated in the contemporary circumstances in which students are daily bombarded with multimodal texts, this chapter provides teacher educators and practitioners with practical steps to apply theory into practice in their classroom and equip all students with the strategies and tools necessary to carry out multimodal discourse analysis (MDA) on picture books.

Picture books play a central role in literacy education in today's elementary classrooms. Usually the entry point for young readers into the field of literacy, picture books are an important part of culture and a noteworthy instrument of socialization (Painter, Martin, & Unsworth, 2013). They are one of the first texts to which children are introduced and continue to be significant in reading and writ-

Expanding Literacy Practices Across Multiple Modes and
Languages for Multilingual Students, pages 1–19
Copyright © 2019 by Information Age Publishing

ing instruction throughout upper grades. Rich with verbal storylines and visual elements, picture books create a unique multimodal, meaning-making experience for readers. Stakeholders in education have recognized the importance of this literary genre, and as early as kindergarten, the Common Core State Standards (CCSS) ask students to describe the relationship between pictures and the story in which they appear (National Governors' Association Center for Best Practices & Council of Chief State School Officers, 2010).

With students constantly being bombarded with multimodal texts outside of school, the conventional idea that literacy only includes written words has been in question for some time. The importance of visual literacy has been explored by several leading scholars in the field (Callow, 2008; Kress & van Leeuwen, 2006; Pantaleo, 2015), with more weight being given to research in this area than ever before. Kress & van Leeuwen (2006) illustrate the magnitude of visual literacy:

> Visual communication is coming to be less and less the domain of specialists, and more and more crucial in the domains of public communication. Inevitably this will lead to new, and more rules, and to more formal, normative teaching. Not being "visually literate" will begin to attract social sanctions. "Visual literacy" will begin to be a matter of survival, especially in the workplace. (p. 3)

Visual images are a critical tool for literacy comprehension (Kress & van Leeuwen, 2006; Lapp, Flood, & Fisher, 1999; Pantaleo, 2015; Serafini, 2010), especially for multilingual students (Gersten & Baker, 2000; Matthews, 2014; Vaughn & Linan-Thompson, 2007). Pictures can provide crucial scaffolding that supports comprehension for students who are reading in a language which is not their first (Bland, 2013). When multilingual students are still developing second-language literacy skills, the images in picture books provide them with an additional meaning-making resource. With the growing number of multilingual students in classrooms across the United States (National Center for Education Statistics, 2016; Sparks, 2016), it becomes even more crucial that educators have the resources to effectively utilize and teach multimodal texts, capitalizing on all they offer. There are underlying complex processes required for reading picture books; modes need to be viewed, read, or processed in combination, as they contain different potentials for making meaning (Kress & van Leeuwen, 2006). These processes need to be explicit for both practitioners and children.

Teachers need to be able to understand the structures and relationships between multimodal elements of picture books so that they can teach diverse students practical, inclusive strategies for comprehension; however, this can be intimidating task. The purpose of this chapter is to offer a brief overview of the theoretical framework that supports multimodal analysis of picture books, to give a concise recount of themes found in research surrounding this topic, to propose a few strategies for classroom teachers, and to discuss implications for literacy teacher education.

THEORETICAL FRAMEWORK

Drawing on the fields of *systemic-functional linguistics* (SFL; de Oliveira & Schleppegrell, 2015; Halliday, 2003; Matthiessen, Lam, & Teruya, 2010; Martin & Rose, 2007) and *visual grammar* (Christie & Unsworth, 2005; Kress & van Leeuwen, 2006; Leborg, 2006), a multimodal analysis of children's picture books is based on the theoretical framework of *multimodal discourse analysis* (MDA; Jewitt, 2009a; Kress, 2000, 2010; O'Halloran, 2004; Painter et al., 2013). SFL, a social semiotic theory that focuses on language and its meaning in applied contexts, contributes to the discourse analysis of verbal elements (Matthiessen et al., 2010). Visual grammar, a framework that linguistically defines and classifies images in terms of objects and structures, patterns and processes, and relationships between the individual elements in the system, assists in analyzing the visual elements (Christie & Unsworth, 2005; Leborg, 2006). MDA brings the verbal and visual elements together for a comprehensive, multimodal analysis of the whole picture book.

MDA recognizes that all modes are culturally given resources for meaning making that are shaped by social interactions (Kress, 2009). When verbal and visual modes are both present in a text (e.g. children's picture books), it is imperative to recognize that neither mode can be completely isolated as a communicative event. The interface between simultaneously present modes creates meaning in a unique way (Jewitt, 2009b); they can interact to highlight a similar message within multiple modes, complement each other while providing additional information, or even offer conflicting messages (Jewitt, 2009b; Smith, 2014; Unsworth, 2006). Furthermore, these multimodal texts are dynamic and interactive, as readers choose where to look and how to engage with the different elements within the text (Hassett & Curwood, 2009; Jewitt, 2009b). The singularity of the MDA framework offers researchers and practitioners the potential to describe semiotic resources for meaning-making, to explore the different affordances of each mode, and to investigate how the individual modes interact in picture books. The following section offers a look at research surrounding multimodal analysis of picture books.

Research on Multimodal Analysis of Children's Picture Books

Method of Review. The goals of this literature review (both conceptual articles and studies) of MDA of image-text relations in printed narrative children's picture books were (a) to identify frameworks and taxonomies used for analyzing image-text relationships in picture books and (b) to identify emerging themes throughout multimodal analyses on picture books. By searching electronic databases using keywords, examining peer-reviewed journals that covered the topics of literacy and multimodality, and mining reference lists, 14 articles that fit the specific study inclusion criteria were identified. In the first stage of the review process, each study was read through the lenses of the two goals. Theoretical frameworks, multimodal analysis taxonomies, and terminology were noted. Next, significant findings from multimodal analyses of picture books were located and compared across the corresponding articles, resulting in the emergence of overarching themes. In the last phase, all articles were reviewed and analyzed for each identified theme, which were then further defined. Five of the articles (Agosto, 1999; Nikolajeva & Scott, 2000; Sipe, 2012; Unsworth, 2006; Wu, 2014) were conceptual articles that presented a theoretical framework for multimodally analyzing children's picture books. Two articles (Serafini, 2010; Sipe, 1998) presented a theoretical framework, but then utilized this to then systematically analyze one or more children's books. Seven articles (Astorga, 1999; Kummerling-Meibauer, 1999; Moya Guijarro, 2010, 2011a, 2011b, 2016; Moya Guijarro & Pinar Sanz, 2008) were composed of MDA that focused on image-text relationships.

FINDINGS

Themes in Multimodal Analysis Frameworks/Taxonomies for Picture Books

The conceptual articles and studies that presented frameworks for multimodal analysis of children's picture books (Agosto, 1999; Nikolajeva & Scott, 2000; Serafini, 2010; Sipe, 1998, 2012; Unsworth, 2006; Wu, 2014) were each unique, composed of different terms and/or taxonomies. Identified terminology to describe relations between visual and verbal modes in picture books could be grouped into two main categories: (a) terms for congruent or symmetrical relationships, and (b) terms for complementary or even contradictory relationships.

Several articles specified overarching terms to refer to the idea of *congruency*. Table 1.1 provides terms and their definitions found throughout the articles, grouped together by the overall idea. All terms are similar in that parallel verbal and visual representations occur, each mode reiterating and reinforcing its counterpart. Within congruency, it is important to recognize that different levels of redundancy exist between the pictures and words (Unsworth, 2006; Wu, 2014). These levels of repetition affect how the meaning is communicated to the reader. The closer that the image and text are to being redundant, the more passive the reader's role is (Nikolajeva & Scott, 2000).

Like congruent terminology, articles also specified overarching terms to refer to the idea of *extension* through complementary and contradictory relationships between verbal and visual modes in picture books. All these terms include a component that discusses how additional information that is not found in one mode is presented in another. Moving along a continuum of semiotic reconstrual, from small differences to drastically singular modes, images and texts work together to extend one another through complementary or contradictory roles (Moya Guijarro, 2016). The elements of multimodal picture books can function concurrently to provide information that is missing in one of the modes, or they can counterpoint one another. The more divergent the relationship between the modes is, the more

TABLE 1.1. Terms Used to Describe Congruent Relationships between Images and Texts

Overall Idea	Terms	Definitions
Overarching Term		
Congruency	Concurrence	The ideational equivalence between image and text, degrees of redundancy (Unsworth, 2006).
	Elaboration	A relationship of similarity across semiotic modes while no new ideational element is introduced by either mode (Wu, 2014).
	Symmetrical interaction	Words and pictures tell the same story, essentially repeating information in different forms of communication (Nikolajeva & Scott, 2000).
	Parallel storytelling	Text and illustrations tell the same stories simultaneously, a "twice-told story" (Agosto, 1999).
Subcategories		
Exposition	Exposition	The image and text are at the same level of generality (subcategory of concurrence; Unsworth, 2006).
		The image and text reinforce each other by restating or reformulating meaning in some way (subcategory of elaboration; Wu, 2014).
Exemplification	Instantiation	The language conveys the habitual nature of the activity, while the image indicates at least one instance or vice versa (subcategory of concurrence; Unsworth, 2006).
	Exemplification	The image exemplifies text or text exemplifies the image; different levels of generality (subcategory of elaboration; Wu, 2014).
Homospatiality	Homospatiality	Refers to texts where two different semiotic modes co-occur in one spatially bonded homogenous entity (subcategory of concurrence; Unsworth, 2006).
		Type of concurrence between image and text, where different semiotic modes co-occur in one spatially bonded homogeneous entity (subcategory of elaboration; Wu, 2014).

complex the text can become. Table 1.2 provides the different terminology and definitions used throughout the articles, grouped together by overall ideas.

Themes in Multimodal Analyses of Picture Books

The following themes emerged throughout the literature including multimodal analyses of children's picture books (Astorga, 1999; Kummerling-Meibauer, 1999; Moya Guijarro, 2010, 2011a, 2011b, 2016; Moya Guijarro & Pinar Sanz, 2008; Serafini, 2010; Sipe, 1998): (a) images are used to present elements of narratives; (b) visual and verbal modalities are generative in meaning making; (c)

TABLE 1.2. Terms Used to Describe Extending Relationships between Images and Texts

Overall Idea	Terms	Definitions
Overarching Term		
	Complementarity	What is represented in images and what is represented in language may be different, but complementary and joint contributors to an overall meaning (Unsworth, 2006).
		Words and pictures reveal semantic gaps that demand mutual completion (Kummerling-Meibauer, 1999).
Extension	Extension	Complementary relations of modalities where image and text complement each other to extend the meaning represented in the other mode (Wu, 2014).
	Enhancing relationship	Pictures amplify more fully the meaning of the words, or vice versa (Kikolajeva & Scott, 2000).
	Interdependent story telling	The reader must consider both forms of media concurrently in order to comprehend the picture book (Agosto, 1999).
Connection	Connection	Connection between images and text (Unsworth, 2006).

Subcategories

Category	Subcategory	Description
Augmentation	Augmentation	Each mode provides meanings additional to and consistent with those in the other mode; one extends the other. (subcategory of complementarity; Unsworth, 2006).
		Image extends or adds new meanings to the text or vice versa by providing additional ideational elements (subcategory of extension; Wu, 2014).
		The texts and illustrations amplify, extend, and complete the story that the other tells. (subcategory of interdependent storytelling; Agosto, 1999).
	Minimal enhancement	Pictures do not add much that is different from the text to the narrative, (subcategory of enhancement; Nikolajeva & Scott, 2000).
	Significant enhancement: Complementary relationship	Pictures and prose rarely overlap, but work together to strengthen the ultimate effect (subcategory of enhancement; Nikolajeva & Scott, 2000).
Divergence	Divergence	Ideational meaning of the text different than that of the image, or vice versa. Instances occur where the meanings across modes contradict each other (subcategory of complementarity, Unsworth, 2006; subcategory of extension, Wu, 2014).
	Counterpoint	The words and images provide alternative information or contradict each other in some way (Nikolajeva & Scott, 2000).
		Two separate stories run in tandem (Kummerling-Meibauer, 1999).
	Contradiction	The texts and illustrations present conflicting information (subcategory of interdependent storytelling; Agosto, 1999).
Projection	Projection	Quoting or reporting of speech or thoughts in speech or thought bubbles (subcategory of connection; Unsworth, 2006; Wu, 2014).
Conjunction	Conjunction	Connection of images and text in terms of casual, temporal, or spatial relations (subcategory of extension; Unsworth, 2006).
	Enhancement	One mode provides meanings which expand another spatially, temporally, or casually (Wu, 2014).
	Distribution	Construction of activity sequences with juxtaposed images and text jointly (sub category of extension; Wu, 2014).

participation is required of the reader; and (d) overtly teaching a metalanguage is important. They are not listed in any particular importance, but rather presented in a way that shows how the themes are all interconnected.

The first theme was images appeared to present different elements of narratives (setting, characters, point of view, mood, temporality) in picture books (Astorga, 1999; Moya Guijarro, 2016; Unsworth, 2006). The pictures were used to enhance and expand the meaning of words, further developing one or more narrative elements. One of the most prevalent ways that images seemed to present elements of narratives was through *visual characterization* (Moya Guijarro, 2016; Unsworth, 2006), through which the illustrations give additional information about the characters. Linguistic attributes and qualities discussed in the text are often represented through actions and behavioral processes (Unsworth, 2006). This visual context helps establish a context for the story and facilitates decoding and comprehension of narrative elements for children, especially multilingual ones.

A second emerging theme is the sum of visual and verbal modalities is greater than merely just the addition of the two modes (Moya Guijarro, 2011a; Nikolajeva & Scott, 2000; Sipe, 1998, 2012; Unsworth, 2006; Wu, 2014). The visual elements are just as important as the verbal elements, and even when the modes appear to be similar, both are necessary to understand the full meaning of a given text. Sometimes the modes can appear to tell two different stories or realities through divergent verbal and visual texts (Moya Guijarro, 2011a; Nikolajeva & Scott, 2000). Whether the modes appear to fall at the congruent or divergent end of the image-text relations spectrum, all picture books demand rereading. The pictures and words contribute to one another in a continuous cycle, constantly helping construct new connections in the other mode and modifying what the reader already knows (Sipe, 1998). The reader becomes a co-creator of meaning and fills in the gaps in one mode with information from the other mode (Nikolajeva & Scott, 2000; Unsworth, 2006; Wu, 2014). This visual-verbal interface is synergistic; the production of the two modes in picture books has a combined effect that is greater than their separate effects (Sipe, 1998, 2012; Unsworth, 2006).

A third theme is the idea of negotiation of meaning between the reader and the text (Agosto, 1999; Kummerling-Meibauer, 1999; Moya Guijarro, 2011a, 2011b; Nikolajeva & Scott, 2000; Sipe, 1998; Unsworth, 2006; Wu, 2014). The previous theme demonstrated that books require interaction from their readers; however, the amount of participation and engagement required by each text varies. When books have more congruent images and verbiage, they tend not to require as much interaction as those that are divergent. As soon as the a mode provides alternative information that deviates from the other, more opportunities for multiple interpretations emerge. Texts with contradictory modes can have several effects (Kummerling-Meibauer, 1999; Nikolajeva & Scott, 2000; Wu, 2014), such as humor, irony, or foreshadowing. They can also maintain children's attention by providing missing information in one mode that was not present in the other mode (Moya Guijarro, 2011b; Sipe, 1998). Concurrently, multimodal picture books require children to interact and evaluate meaning created by the text, based on their own experiences. The reader assumes an interactive role as he or she contemplates an image that demands a response (Unsworth, 2006).

The first three themes demonstrate that images and words work together with the interactive reader to create meaning, resulting in the fourth theme: In order for readers to be able to effectively analyze the relationship between the verbal and visual elements, it is crucial to develop a common metalanguage for talking about books (Astorga, 1999; Unsworth, 2006). Picture books can be analyzed in a variety of ways, such as focusing on the presentation of ideas, the enactment of a relationship with the reader, or the construction of a cohesive message. They can be examined at different levels and from different perspectives, such as the reader describing the multimodal text, interpreting compositions and how they create meaning, or interpreting it within a social context (Astorga, 1999; Serafini, 2010). With this myriad of analytical methods and perspectives through which to explore multimodal texts, it is apparent that it is important to develop and implement a common metalanguage that will facilitate the metatextual awareness of image/text relations.

EXPANDING LITERACY PRACTICES: CLASSROOM STRATEGIES

Based on the research surrounding multimodal analysis of children's picture books, this section outlines three specific strategies that educators can use in the classroom to expand literacy practices to support students by providing them with the necessary tools to approach picture books. Effective strategy instruction includes explicitly naming and describing the strategy; modeling the strategy; and providing various levels of scaffolding opportunities for students to use the strategy (Calkins, 2015; Duke, Pearson, Strachan, & Billman, 2011).

One way that educators can teach each strategies is through a mini-lesson, followed by a time for independent practice (Calkins, 2015). This provides students with multiple occasions to work collaboratively and independently, while affording teachers the opportunity to differentiate instruction. All classrooms contain students with individual needs, and this format is especially conducive to classes composed of multilingual students with a range of language proficiency levels. Each strategy outlined below is accompanied by a sample lesson that includes direct, explicit instruction. All lessons are designed for a third-grade classroom, but could be easily adapted for a different grade.

Strategy One: Readers Use a Specific Language to Talk about Pictures and Words

It is important to overtly teach the metalanguage necessary for analyzing image-text relations in picture books to ensure terms for discussing and analyzing multimodal texts have a shared meaning. Without this common language, classroom discussions will not be effective, and meaning can be lost. Therefore, this is one of the first steps when examining picture books from a multimodal perspective.

As described earlier in this chapter, there is a plethora of terminology used to describe MDA in picture books. While educators may want to develop their own metalanguage to use with students when analyzing the relationships between verbal and visual elements, I strongly suggest developing a metalanguage that is common throughout the school. Research has shown the critical importance of a common language of instruction (Schooling, Toth, & Marzano, 2013). This allows students to carry this metalanguage with them from one grade to the next, minimizing confusion and extra time spent relearning new terminology each year. The example lesson in Table 1.3 demonstrates how terms and definitions could be explicitly taught in an elementary classroom.

TABLE 1.3. Example Lesson #1

Lesson Title: Readers Use a Specific Language to Talk about Pictures and Words

Target Grade: 3rd

Mini-lesson	*Connection:* Gather the students together and discuss how people need to speak the same language to understand one another, giving engaging examples of what might happen if there wasn't common understanding.
	Teaching: Tell the students that you want to teach them that readers use a specific language—a metalanguage—when talking about the pictures and words in picture books. Start an anchor chart that shows the common language your class will use.

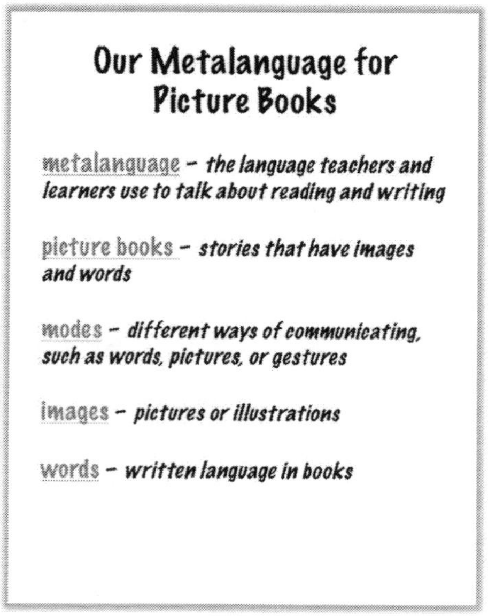

Our Metalanguage for Picture Books

metalanguage – *the language teachers and learners use to talk about reading and writing*

picture books – *stories that have images and words*

modes – *different ways of communicating, such as words, pictures, or gestures*

images – *pictures or illustrations*

words – *written language in books*

FIGURE 1.1. Example metalanguage anchor chart.

TABLE 1.3.   Continued

	Active Engagement: Have students turn to a partner and practice describing an image using as many terms from the anchor chart as possible. Listen in to the students and have a couple share their descriptions utilizing metalanguage.
	Link: Tell the students that they are going to get the opportunity to practice this during their independent reading time today. They need to come up with at least three sentences that describe their books, using terms from the anchor chart.
Independent Practice	Send students off to their reading spots with their own individual books. During this time, they are reading independently and recording their metalanguage examples in their reading journals.
	Use this time to confer with individual students or small groups, scaffolding them in this strategy and other previous reading strategies.
Closing/ Sharing	Bring the class back together and allow students to share an example of how they used the metalanguage to describe their books today.
	Remind them that you will continue to add to this anchor chart, as you learn more about how images and words work together.

Strategy Two: Readers Pay Attention to how Images and Words Interact

Once a metalanguage for talking about picture books is established, it is important to explicitly teach students how to analyze the relationship between verbal and visual elements in picture books. Teachers can help develop active readers through this strategy through the following steps: (a) teaching the students about the different types of relationships that images and words can have, (b) modeling how to analyze the type of relationship, and (c) supporting students practicing this strategy in small groups. The lesson in Table 1.4 demonstrates one way that teachers could implement this strategy in their classroom.

Strategy Three: Readers Find Evidence in Images and Words

A third strategy to expand literacy practices in the classroom is to teach students how to use both images and words to provide evidence for their statements about text. There is currently a push towards text-based evidence (Cherry-Paul & Johansen, 2014), and students can use both visual and verbal elements of texts to provide substantiation for their statements. The lesson plan in Table 1.5 gives an example of how to do teach this strategy to students.

TABLE 1.4.   Example Lesson #2

Lesson Title: Readers Pay Attention to how Images and Words Interact

Target Grade: 3rd

Mini-lesson   *Connection:* Remind students about the special metalanguage for talking about picture books. Show them and image with a sentence that similar to a picture. Then show them the same image with a sentence that is different from the picture. Ask them what the main difference is between the two options. Ask them if it would be possible for each to image/text combination to be a page in a picture book.

Example image-text relationships:

FIGURE 1.2. Image-text relationship showing similarity (Campbell, 2017).

FIGURE 1.3. Image-text relationship showing difference.

Teaching: Tell the students you want to teach them that images and words in picture books interact in different ways. Sometimes they are similar, and sometimes they are different. Start an anchor chart that shows the different relationships between images and words.

TABLE 1.4. Continued

> ## Relationships Between Images and Words
>
> similar relationships:
> **the words and images show the same thing**
> -
> repetition- **the words and image repeat each other**
>
> "One day, Angus attacked his sister."
>
> example - **one mode gives an example of the other one**
>
> "Angus was always pouncing on his sister."
>
> different relationships:
> **the words and image do not show the same thing**
> -
> addition - **new meaning is provided by the words or images**
>
> "Angus liked to entertain himself."
>
> contradiction- **the words and pictures have opposite meanings**
>
> "Angus was a very well-behaved kitten."

FIGURE 1.4. Example anchor chart for image-text relationships.

Model for students how you can analyze a picture or two from a familiar picture book. Remind them to use the metalanguage.

Active Engagement: Have students work with a partner to practice analyzing the multimodal relationship in another familiar picture book. Listen to the students and encourage a couple of them share their analyses.

Link: Tell the students that they are going to get the opportunity to practice this themselves during their independent reading time today. They need to come up with an analysis for at least three sets of images and words from their own picture books.

Independent Practice

Students go off to their reading spots. During this time, they are reading independently and recording their image and word relationship analyses in their reading journals. You can supply the children with a personal-sized copy of the anchor chart for their reference.

Use this time to confer with individual students or small groups, scaffolding them in this strategy and previous reading strategies that they have learned.

Closing/ Sharing

Bring the class back together, and have students share their own analysis example from their reading time. Try to encourage a diversity of answers (similar and different relationships) and add some of these to the anchor chart that you made in the mini-lesson.

TABLE 1.5. Example Lesson #3

Lesson Title: Readers Find Evidence in Images and Words

Target Grade: 3rd

Mini-lesson	*Connection:* Gather the students together and talk with them about how it's not enough for lawyers to claim something; they must also show proof.

Teaching: Tell the students that you want to teach them that readers find proof, or evidence, for their claims in both pictures and words. Start an anchor chart that shows sentence stems and examples the students could use.

Readers Find Evidence in Images & Words

Example Question: How was Angus feeling?

I know ____ because the text said...
"I know Angus was was sad, because the text said that a tear ran down his face."

The author stated... This tells me...
"The author stated that Angus was crying. This tells me that he was sad."

The image shows...
"The image shows a tear on Angus' face. This demonstrates that he was sad."

An example of this is on page __, when...
"Angus was sad. An example of this is on page 11, when it says he has a tear on his face."

This is clear in the picture because...
"Angus is sad. This is clear in the picture because there is a tear in his eye."

FIGURE 1.5. Example anchor chart for text-based evidence from images and words.

Demonstrate making a couple claims about a picture book, utilizing evidence from the images and pictures.

Active Engagement: Have students turn to each other and practice making a couple claims about another picture book with which they are all familiar. Listen in to the students and have a couple share their claims, supported by evidence.

Link: Tell the students that they are going to get the opportunity to practice this themselves during their independent reading time today. They need to come up with at least three claims that describe their picture books and support them with evidence from the text.

TABLE 1.5. Continued

Independent Practice	Students go off to their reading spots. During this time, they are reading independently and recording their claims and evidence in their reading journals.
	Use this time to confer with individual students or small groups, scaffolding them in this strategy and previous reading strategies that they have learned.
Closing/ Sharing	Bring the class back together, and have each student share a claim and the supporting evidence from the verbal or visual elements of text.

IMPLICATIONS FOR LITERACY TEACHER EDUCATION

The goal of the research in this chapter was to synthesize literature on multimodal analysis of children's picture books, in order to understand the current taxonomies and metalanguage being used by scholars and to understand ways multimodality in picture books is currently being assessed. This research on multimodal analysis of children's picture books revealed that it is still a developing field, with still a paucity of published articles. A theme that was identified across terminology describing image/text relationships showed that most terms are used to either describe congruent relationships, or to describe complementary or contradictory relationships. Articles that analyzed the multimodality of picture books produced another four themes, demonstrating that both the verbal and visual modes function together to create a result that is greater than the sum of the individual modes. This literature also illustrated that participation is required of the reader, and that the amount of participation required often falls along a continuum. Finally, the variety of perspectives from which picture books can be multimodally analyzed, combined with the wide variety of terms used to describe image/text relationships, demonstrated how it is necessary to develop a common metalanguage.

These central findings on multimodal analysis of children's books reveal how important the image/text relationship is for reading comprehension, and therefore teachers need to be educated about this relationship and given strategies to help their students understand it. All texts are interpreted by the reader, and meaning is co-created. It becomes clear that practitioners have the responsibility to teach explicitly children not only aspects of visual literacy, but also how to use multiple modes while reading. Children can utilize the separate modes to help support their comprehension. Astorga (1999) suggests that ELL students could greatly benefit from learning how to utilize both modes in children literature. Since books require a continuum of participation from the reader, based on the complexity in the relationship between image and text, it is important for teachers to keep that in mind when helping young readers choose books. The challenge of divergent pictures and words may engage some students, but it may confuse a student who has not developed strong language skills. They can also decide on the levels of complexity and of interaction that they want to require from the reader.

In order to teach children about image/text relationships, it is also essential for practitioners to overtly teach children a metalanguage, or a way to talk about text. A commitment from practitioners and students to understanding and utilizing a metalanguage (Unsworth, 2006) is promising for classroom discussions that can engage children in critical discourse analysis (Rogers & Mosley Wetzel, 2014), even at a young age. These discussions can also foster more than just reading comprehension. Picture books are a great resource to use as mentor texts (Dean & Grierson, 2005; Laminack & Wadsworth, 2015; Shubitz, 2016) to teach children how to create their own narrative. Explicit instruction about the elements of a narrative, often represented multimodally, can help children understand how they can use those features in their own writing.

Teachers are essential for bringing research into the classroom, both to test hypotheses and to implement recent developments in knowledge in a practical way. With this topic still in its infancy, there is much to be learned about image/text relationships and multimodal analysis of picture books. This provides researchers, teacher educators, and practitioners alike a great opportunity to collaborate to investigate, theorize, and re-define the idea of literacy to inform practical, effective pedagogy.

REFLECTION QUESTIONS

1. How could you envision using image-text relationships in picture books in your classroom?
2. How could you expand the strategies presented in this chapter to include other types of multimodal resources?
3. What terminology do you think is important to include when developing a metalanguage for analyzing image-text relationships in picture books?
4. What do you think is the next step for future research regarding multimodal analysis of picture books?

REFERENCES

Agosto, D. E. (1999). One and inseparable: Interdependent storytelling in picture storybooks. *Children's Literature in Education, 30*(4), 267–280. doi:10.1023/A:1022471922077

Astorga, M. C. (1999). The text-image interaction and second language learning. *Australian Journal of Language and Literacy, 22*(3), 212–233.

Bland, J. (2013). *Children's literature and learner empowerment: Children and teenagers in English language education.* New York, NY: Bloomsbury.

Calkins, L. (2015). *A guide to the reading workshop.* Portsmouth, NH: Heinemann.

Callow, J. (2008). Show me: Principles for assessing students' visual literacy. *The Reading Teacher, 61*(8), 616–626. doi:10.1598/RT.61.8.3

Campbell, T. (Photographer). (2017, March 20). *Cute kittens leaping and playing* [digital image]. Retrieved from https://stock.adobe.com/stock-photo/cute-kittens-leaping-and-playing/133137992

Cherry-Paul, S., & Johansen, D. (2014). *Teaching interpretation using text-based evidence to construct meaning.* Portsmouth, NH: Heinemann.

Christie, F., & Unsworth, L. (2005). Developing socially responsible language research. In L. Unsworth (Ed.), *Researching language in schools and communities: Functional linguistic perspectives* (pp. 1–26). London, UK: Continuum.

de Oliveira, L. C., & Schleppegrell, M. J. (2015). *Focus on grammar and meaning.* Oxford, UK: Oxford University Press.

Dean, D., & Grierson, S. (2005). Re-envisioning reading and writing through combined-text picture books. *Journal of Adolescent and Adult Literacy, 48*(6), 456–468.

Duke, N. K., Pearson, P. D., Strachan, S. L., & Billman, A. K. (2011). Essential elements of fostering and teaching reading comprehension. In S. J. Samuels & A. E. Farstrup (Eds.), *What research has to say about reading instruction* (4th ed., pp. 51–93). Newark, DE: International Reading Association.

Gersten, R., & Baker, S. (2000). What we know about effective instructional practices for English-language learners. *Exceptional Children, 66*(4), 454–470. doi:10.1177/001440290006600402

Hassett, D. D., & Curwood, J. S. (2009). Theories and practices of multimodal education: The instructional dynamics of picture books and primary classrooms. *The Reading Teacher, 63*(4), 270–282. doi:10.1598/RT.63.4.2

Halliday, M. A. K. (2003). *Collected works of M. A. K. Halliday: On language and linguistics* (Vol. 3). New York, NY: Continuum.

Jewitt, C. (Ed.). (2009a). *The Routledge handbook of multimodal analysis.* New York, NY: Routledge.

Jewitt, C. (2009b). An introduction to multimodality. In C. Jewitt (Ed.), *The Routledge handbook of multimodal analysis* (pp. 14–27). New York, NY: Routledge.

Kress, G. (2000). Multimodality: Challenges to thinking about language. *TESOL Quarterly, 34*(2), 337–340. doi:10.2307/3587959

Kress, G. (2009). What is mode? In C. Jewitt (Ed.), *The Routledge handbook of multimodal analysis* (pp. 54–67). New York, NY: Routledge.

Kress, G. (2010). *Multimodality: A social semiotic approach to contemporary communication.* New York, NY: Routledge.

Kress, G., & van Leeuwen, T. (2006). *Reading images: The grammar of visual design* (2nd ed.). New York, NY: Routledge.

Kümmerling-Melbauer, B. (1999). Metalinguistic awareness and the child's developing concept of irony: The relationship between pictures and text in ironic picture books. *The Lion and the Unicorn, 23*(2), 157–183.

Laminack, L. L., & Wadsworth, R. M. (2014). *Writers are readers: Flipping reading instruction into writing opportunities.* Portsmouth, NH: Heinemann.

Lapp, D., Flood, J., & Fisher, D. (1999). Visual literacy: Intermediality: How the use of multiple media enhances learning. *The Reading Teacher, 52*(7), 776–780.

Leborg, C. (2006). *Visual grammar.* New York, NY: Princeton Architectural Press.

Matthews, S. A. (2014). Reading without words: Using *The Arrival* to teach visual literacy with English language learners. *The Clearing House, 87,* 64–68. doi:10.1080/00098655.2013.843499

Matthiessen, C. M. I. M., Lam, M., & Teruya, K. (2010). *Key terms in systemic functional linguistics.* New York, NY: Continuum.

Martin, J. R., & Rose, D. (2007). *Working with discourse: Meaning beyond the clause* (2nd ed.). London, UK: Continuum.

Moya Guijarro, A. J. (2010). A multimodal analysis of *The Tale of Peter Rabbit* within the interpersonal metafunction. *ATLANTIS: Journal of the Spanish Association of Anglo-American Studies, 32*(1), 123–140.

Moya Guijarro, A. J. (2011a). Engaging readers through language and pictures: A case study. *Journal of Pragmatics, 43*, 2982–2991. doi:10.1016/j.pragma.2011.05.012

Moya Guijarro, A. J. (2011b). A bi-modal and systemic-functional study of *Dear Zoo* within the textual metafunction. *Revista Canaria de Estudios Ingleses, 62*, 123–138.

Moya Guijarro, A. J. (2016). The role of semiotic metaphor in the verbal-visual interplay of three children's picture books: A multisemiotic systemic-functional approach. *Journal of the Spanish Association of Anglo-American Studies, 38*(1), 33–52.

Moya Guijarro, J., & Pinar Zanz, M. J. (2008). Compositional, interpersonal, and representational meanings in a children's narrative: A multimodal discourse analysis. *Journal of Pragmatics, 40*, 1601–1619. doi:10.1016/j.pragma.2008.04.019

National Center for Education Statistics. (2016). *The condition of education: English language learners in public schools.* Washington, DC: National Center for Education Statistics. Retrieved from https://nces.ed.gov/programs/coe/indicator_cgf.asp

National Governors Association Center for Best Practices, Council of Chief State School Officers. (2010). *Common core state standards for English language arts and literacy in history/social studies, science, and technical subjects.* Washington, DC: National Governors Association Center for Best Practices, Council of Chief State School Officers. Retrieved from http://www.corestandards.org/ELA-Literacy/

Nikolajeva, M., & Scott, C. (2000). The dynamics of picturebook communication. *Children's Literature in Education, 31*(4), 225–239.

O'Halloran, K. (Ed.). (2004). *Multimodal discourse analysis: Systemic functional perspectives.* New York, NY: Continuum.

Painter, C., Martin, J. R., & Unsworth, L. (2013). *Reading visual narratives: Image analysis of children's picture books.* Bristol, CT: Equinox.

Pantaleo, S. (2015). Language, literacy and visual texts. *English in Education, 49*(2), 113–129. doi:10.1111/eie.12053

Rogers, R. L., & Mosley Wetzel, M. (2014). *Designing critical literacy education through critical discourse analysis: Pedagogical and research tools for teacher researchers.* New York, NY: Routledge.

Schooling, P., Toth, M., & Marzano, R. (2013). *The critical importance of a common language of instruction.* Blairsville, PA: Learning Sciences International. Retrieved from http://www.marzanocenter.com/files/Common%20Language%20of%20Instruction%5B1%5D.pdf

Serafini, F. (2010). Reading multimodal texts: Perceptual, structural, and ideological perspectives. *Children's Literature in Education, 41*, 85–104. doi:10.1007/s10583-010-9100-5

Sipe, L. R. (1998). How picture books work: A semiotically framed theory of text-picture relationships. *Children's Literature in Education, 29*(2), 97–108. doi:10.1023/A:1022459009182

Sipe, L. R. (2012). Revisiting the relationships between text and pictures. *Children's Literature in Education, 43*, 4–21. doi:10.1007/s10583-011-9153-0

Smith, B. E. (2014). Beyond words: A review of research on adolescents and multimodal composition. In R. E. Ferdig & K. E. Pytash (Eds.). *Exploring multimodal composition and digital writing* (pp. 1–19). Hershey, PA: IGI Global.

Shubitz, S. (2016). *Craft moves: Lesson sets for teaching writing with mentor texts.* Portland, ME: Stenhouse.

Sparks, S. D. (2016). Teaching English-language learners: What does the research tell us? *Education Week, 35*(30), s3–s6. Retrieved from http://www.edweek.org/ew/articles/2016/05/11/teaching-english-language-learners-what-does-the-research.html

Unsworth, L. (2006). Towards a metalanguage for multiliteracies education: Describing the meaning—Making resources of language-image interaction. *English Teaching: Practice and Critique, 5*(1), 55–76.

Vaughn, S., & Linan-Thompson, S. (2007*). Research-based methods of reading instruction for English language learners, grades K–4.* Alexandria, VA: ASCD.

Wu, S. (2014). A multimodal analysis of image-text relations in picture books. *Theory and Practice in Language Studies, 4*(7), 1415–1420. doi:10.4304/tpls.4.7.1415–1420

CHAPTER 2

EXPLORING MULTIMODAL REPRESENTATIONS OF WORDS IN A FOURTH-GRADE ENGLISH LANGUAGE ARTS TEACHER GUIDE TO SUPPORT EMERGENT BILINGUALS' VOCABULARY INSTRUCTION

Irina Malova, Alain Bengochea, Susan R. Massey, and Mary A. Avalos

Current rigorous learning standards position vocabulary learning and knowledge as crucial for comprehension of complex texts, specifically for emergent bilinguals, or those who have a potential to develop a bilingual proficiency. Drawing on results of vocabulary instruction and learning activities for EBs from a recent content analysis of a fourth-grade English Language Arts teacher's guide, this chapter describes how multimodal texts (texts with different types of media used–visuals, gestures, sounds) are designed to support learning about words during whole-group lessons. Additionally, we provide suggestions for extending the use of multimodal resources and approaches beyond the teacher's guide to support

Expanding Literacy Practices Across Multiple Modes and
Languages for Multilingual Students, pages 21–37.
Copyright © 2019 by Information Age Publishing
All rights of reproduction in any form reserved.

EBs' English vocabulary learning using an established framework for multimodal instruction.

This chapter examines the directives involving multimodal representations of words found in a basal reading program's teacher's guide (TG) designed to support the implementation of the Common Core State Standards (CCSS for English Language Arts [ELA]/Literacy; National Governors Association Center for Best Practices [NGA] & Council of Chief State School Officers [CCSSO], 2010a). Specifically, we explore the suggested teacher instructional moves utilizing multimodal representations that may serve to support English Language Learners' (ELLs) vocabulary instruction. In this study, we define multimodal representations as a variety of modes (verbal, actional, spatial, and visual) used during vocabulary instruction. The steady increase of ELLs' nationwide enrollment demands greater attention to issues of education involving diverse cultural and linguistic groups. In this chapter, we refer to ELLs as *emergent bilinguals* (EBs) (Garcia, 2009) to highlight learners' potential to develop bilingual proficiency through sustained exposure to and support of multiple languages and to underscore the inextricable nature of their linguistic and cultural knowledge across their languages (García, 1983; García, 2009; Garcia, Kleifgen, & Falchi, 2008; Reyes, 2006).

In light of the growing number of EBs, it is important to examine the means of improving instruction for both non-EB and EB students in the context of the (National Governor's Association Center for Best Practices and Council of Chief State School Officers, 2010a) adopted by 42 states in the United States. English Language Arts (ELA) CCSS directs educators to assess the performance of students in reading, writing, and vocabulary. In particular, language standards for kindergarten through fifth grade in the CCSS (NGA & CCSSO, 2010a) emphasize what is expected from students in terms of vocabulary acquisition and use:

- Determine or clarify the meaning of unknown and multiple-meaning words and phrases based on grade 4 reading and content, choosing flexibly from a range of strategies (Standard 4.4).
- Demonstrate understanding of figurative language, word relationships, and nuances in word meanings (Standard 4.5).
- Acquire and use accurately grade-appropriate general academic and domain-specific words and phrases, including those that signal precise actions, emotions, or states of being (e.g., quizzed, whined, stammered) and that are basic to a particular topic (e.g., *wildlife, conservation,* and *endangered* when discussing animal preservation) (Standard 4.6).

In alignment with these standards, current research indicates that vocabulary knowledge is a crucially significant factor for competent receptive and productive communication in a first and second language (Dockrell, Stuart, & King, 2010). Since the report from the National Reading Panel (2000), there has been a growing volume of research focusing on vocabulary instruction with monolingual children (Biemiller & Boote, 2006; Hargrave & Senechal, 2000; Marulis &

Neuman, 2010). However, there still remains disproportionate research focusing on vocabulary instructional methods for EBs. Despite the scant research on how best to teach EBs, there is a wide consensus that disproportionate English vocabulary knowledge between EBs and their monolingual counterparts can impact EBs' reading proficiency and comprehension (August & Shanahan, 2006; Carlo et al., 2004).

Vocabulary acquisition is an ongoing, multifaceted, and multimodal process (Carlo et al., 2004; Nation, 2013; Silverman, 2007). Verbal, actional, spatial, and visual modes, which may include the use of gestures, role play, facial expressions, particular classroom configurations (e.g., writing center, dramatic play area) and objects (e.g., realia, child-signified artifacts), may serve as resources for meaning-making in a shared community (Norris, 2004). With this in mind, multimodal representations can be incorporated in intentional ways to promote vocabulary learning, especially among EBs who may require additional vocabulary scaffolds (Echevarria, Vogt, & Short, 2013; Graves, August, & Mancilla-Martinez, 2012; Nation, 2013). This study explores the recommendations, embedded within a 4th grade post-CCSS TG, for employing multimodal representations during vocabulary instruction.

LITERATURE REVIEW

Because EBs may navigate two or more language systems while advancing through grade-level content that becomes increasingly complex, they may expectedly require additional or different instructional support than their monolingual peers (Gersten & Baker, 2000; Gersten & Geva, 2003; Moats, 2001). During comprehension-oriented reading tasks, all learners are expected to engage lower-level (e.g., phonemic awareness, decoding, phonics, fluency) and higher-level skills (e.g., inferencing, vocabulary knowledge). Although lower-level skills (or word reading skills) generally are well-developed by the middle elementary grades for EBs, vocabulary differentials remain between EBs and their native English-speaking peers due to fewer opportunities for exposure to their second-language (L2) vocabulary (August & Shanahan, 2006). As such, vocabulary acquisition becomes critical to accelerating their learning and minimizing these differences. Due to the significance of vocabulary in long-term reading achievement (August & Shanahan, 2006), instructional frameworks centering on vocabulary have been proposed to support EBs in particular (Echevarria, Vogt, & Short, 2013; Graves, August, & Mancilla-Martinez, 2012; Nation, 2013). This work has showcased the integration of available multimodal resources to improve both word-reading and word-meaning acquisition. For instance, Nation's (2013) framework focuses on various dimensions of knowing a word and highlights the importance of teaching about the form, meaning, and use of words as a means of enhancing learners' depth of word knowledge.

Although instructional frameworks designed for teaching vocabulary are available, there are relatively few studies that have included multidimensional vocabulary instructional approaches that integrate various modes of communication. In particular, certain studies solely focus on teacher's use of verbal modes during instruction to enhance EBs' vocabulary learning in early and middle childhood (Lugo-Neris, Jackson, & Goldstein, 2010; Ulanoff & Pucci, 1999). Of the few studies solely exploring vocabulary instructional moves through teachers' verbal modes, Lugo-Neris, Jackson, and Goldstein (2010) uniquely showcased the importance of EBs' home language as an additional verbal modal resource for preschool-age, Spanish-English EBs' learning. They highlighted the additional benefits of using Spanish definitional expansions during an English shared book reading as it improved receptive and expressive definitional knowledge of target vocabulary. Most notably, additional vocabulary supports in Spanish showed greater improvements for EBs' learning than solely listening to definitional content in English, which is consistent with other research highlighting the importance of bridging EBs' vocabulary-related understandings through home language supports (Carlo et al, 2004; Ulanoff & Pucci, 1999).

To evaluate the effectiveness of providing a combination of vocabulary instructional moves or strategies in support of EBs' learning, certain experimental studies in early and middle child have embedded vocabulary supports that require teachers to use multiple modes (e.g., manipulating realia, showing illustrations, gesturing). That is, some studies are multi-componential intervention studies designed to provide multifaceted instructional approaches to support vocabulary learning using verbal, actional, and visual modes (Collins, 2004; Dockrell, Stuard, & King, 2010). For instance, Collins (2004) implemented a teacher-directed instructional approach in which rich definitional knowledge was verbally supplied to EBs to improve vocabulary learning. In addition, teachers were requested to point to an illustration of a target word during shared readings (e.g., by pointing to a picture showing the character jumping out of bed and *donning* slippers) and, subsequently in the story, would make a gesture to further students' vocabulary knowledge (e.g., imitating the motion of putting socks and shoes on her feet to explain the action, *to don*), thereby drawing on verbal (i.e., oral language use), actional (i.e., gestures and pointing), and visual modes (i.e., displaying illustrations) to support vocabulary learning. Similarly, other multi-componential, multimodal studies seeking to support EBs' vocabulary learning have included opportunities within as well as beyond shared readings to promote multiple encounters with target vocabulary. These have included print-based activities in which learners engage with visual modes as an additional means of enhancing vocabulary knowledge (Carlo et al., 2004; Nelson, Valdasy, & Sanders, 2011). Teachers of EB kindergartners in Nelson et al.'s (2011) vocabulary-focused intervention study taught definitions through pictures in conjunction with decoding in the reading of short passages with students and learning about synonyms throughout short thematic activities, whereas the control group solely experienced a shared reading. In this study, EBs improved on acquiring targeted words, indicating that there may be an advantage in linking supplemental vocabulary instruction with phonics for EBs.

Similarly, to increase learner autonomy and enhance independent word learning, many interventions reinforced the use of generative vocabulary strategies. By adopting these methods in vocabulary-focused interventions, students were able to engage in certain practices that could potentially lead to incidental vocabulary acquisition and less reliance on teacher support. One such method was providing EBs with opportunities to utilize dictionaries, engaging with visual modes as a resource, to access multiple meanings of words and learn about the importance of selecting appropriate definitions to fit the learning context (Carlo et al., 2004; Proctor et al., 2009). In the same vein, EBs were able to use their visual and verbal modes to further their understandings and potentially and incidentally learn target words by previewing Spanish versions and receiving audio support of an English read aloud later read in class during whole group instruction (Carlo et al., 2004).

Other recent studies indicate that the use of images supports university students' L2 vocabulary leaning and retention (Bisson, Van Heuven, Conklin & Tunney, 2014; Carpenter & Olson, 2012; Kost, Foss, & Lenzini, 1999; Plass, Chun, Mayer & Leutner (1998); Syrodenko, 2010). Bisson and colleagues (2014) reported that when students at the beginning language proficiency were exposed to visual, reading, written, and aural modes, they were able to incidentally acquire foreign language vocabulary. Similary, Royce (2002) stated that the use of visual representation activates cognitive associations that facilitate vocabulary learning.

Regarding the integrated use of multiple modes, Dubois and Vial (2000) investigated whether Russian language students speaking French would recall vocabulary better when it is simultaneously or individually presented in visual and verbal modes. The results of their study indicated that presentation of information in only visual form (image and text) leads to less learning than information presented in visual and verbal form. They contend that "when textual, visual, and auditory materials are integrated in this way, the learner may be forced to engage in additional processing that leads to better memorization" (p. 159).

Similar to the limited volume of research on vocabulary instruction with EBs, there is also a lack of consensus on the most effective methods for teaching vocabulary to these learners. Due to the multi-componential, multimodal nature of most of the cited studies in this review and the challenges in disentangling the effects of individual conditions in the available literature on vocabulary instruction, there is no clear indication of teachers' modal choices used to improve the breadth and depth of EBs' vocabulary. To this point, however, reviews of the literature have provided guidance and emphasized that EBs should be afforded opportunities that promote word consciousness, such as creating word-rich environments in the classroom that prioritizes teaching individual words and word-learning strategies (August & Shanahan, 2006; Graves, August, & Mancilla-Martinez, 2012), which could engage all learners' available modes. Similarly, instructional frameworks for EBs (Echevarria, Vogt, & Short, 2013; Howard, Sugarman, & Coburn, 2006) provide guidelines to teachers on how best to approach vocabulary instruction through certain modifications that differentially engage modes for EBs—e.g., using speech that is appropriate for students' proficiency level; clarifying words and concomitant concepts through text or peer discussions using the non-language of instruction; and providing hands-on materials or manipulatives to practice using new content vocabulary.

THEORETICAL FRAMEWORK

This content analysis is informed by Paivio and Sadoski's (2001) framework of Dual Coding Theory, which underscores that learning events can be enhanced by supporting two separate linguistic and extra-linguistic coding systems. According to Paivio and Sadoski, our mental representations register features and qualities of our experiences. With this in mind, mental representations are captured across two modalities—verbal and non-verbal. Each system has representational units: 1) a verbal unit comprising phonemes, morphemes, or words; and 2) non-verbal units such as images or gestures. According to Paivio and Sadoski (2001), verbal units or words are organized hierarchically within a verbal system, whereas images, opposite to words, are in a linear relationship with each other. Paivio and colleagues suggest four levels of information processing, such as sensory storage system (untransformed information for a short period following stimulus of presentation), representational processes, referential, and associative chains or structures (Clark & Pavio, 1991; Paivio & Sadoski, 2011; Sadoski & Paivio 2001, 2004). Solely the last three levels, which are linked to meaning, will be discussed and used as the analytic lens for this study. The framework described here will guide our analysis of different modes used during vocabulary instruction and the level of support for EBs' vocabulary acquisition, provided by the explicit instructional supports outlined in a teacher's guides. As such, we may only assume which cognitive processes are supported during actual classroom instruction. Thus, guiding our analysis, we refer to Paivio and Sadoski's (2001) three cognitive processes as three types of *scaffolds*, designed for the explicit and direct usage by teachers in reading basal programs. Below are short characteristics of each type of instructional scaffold:

Representational scaffolds correspond to supports provided to learners to become familiar with a novel stimulus, in this case a word. Representational scaffolds aim to support the simple recognition of words and do not facilitate meaning-based learning (Sadoski & Paivio, 2004). A verbal representation unit can be a phoneme, a syllable, a word, depending on what is being used as a functional unit of speech.

Referential scaffolds involve facilitating the interconnections between two systems—verbal and non-verbal—to engage learners in naming a word after a visual stimulus or conjure an image after naming a word. As indicated by Paivio and Sadoski (2001), a word can be used to evoke images and vice versa.

Lastly, *associative scaffolds* create interconnections and structures that involve different categories within a verbal or a visual system. Associative structures can be hierarchically organized (nested sets), where a stimulus leads to a group of words or images, which in turn belong to another group of interrelated words and images. An example of associative scaffolding is reading the written form *cup*, which activates verbal or actional modes, such as uttering the sounds in the word *cup* or gesturing as if taking a sip of an absent cup. In a similar way, an image of a cup can be associated with images of a spoon, saucer, coffee or other items in a kitchen. As it can be seen, associative processing deals with meaningful comprehension within one isolated system—verbal or visual.

In this chapter, we will use Sadoski and Paivio's (2001) framework to gain an understanding of the levels of multimodal, vocabulary-focused scaffolds being suggested for teachers' use in a 4th grade English Language Arts reading basal program. As such, we will identify the types of instructional scaffolds (i.e., representational, referential, and associative) found in the TG's instructional blocks related to vocabulary instruction. Through an in-depth content analysis of one post-CCSS TG, we will learn how teachers are suggested to incorporate verbal and visual representations of words as per dual coding theory.

With this framing, this study will address the following research questions:

1.   What types of multimodal representations are available in 4th grade ELA TG to support vocabulary instruction?
2.   How do (extra-)verbal modes support instruction of word depth?
     a.   How are the instructional directives in the TG geared toward supporting EBs?

METHOD

We examined how the fourth-grade ELA TG of a commercially available basal reading series support vocabulary instruction with multimodal representations (e.g., pictures, gestures, supplemental audiovisual materials), with a particular attention paid to learning supports for EBs. The analyzed post-CCSS TG is currently used in a large metropolitan district in the southeastern U.S. The methods of this study are described below.

The first part of our qualitative analysis was conducted as part of a larger study (Avalos, Malova, Massey, & Bengochea, 2016), where we compared the suggested vocabulary instruction as designed in three TGs (two pre-CCSS and one post-CCSS). Within the scope of a larger study, three instructional units from each TG (beginning, middle, and end of year; five days of instruction per unit, per TG) were chosen to capture the nature of vocabulary instruction and learning. Using content analysis methods when coding the TGs (Bazerman, 2006), we coded three instructional units in each TG focusing on suggested vocabulary instruction and additional support for EBs (as referred to in TGs) at different levels of proficiency (EB beginning, intermediate, and advanced) during whole-class instruction. Each block of instructional vocabulary instruction was coded line by line with a focus on suggested teachers' instructional moves. Three of the four authors coded all pages with vocabulary instruction extracted from three units from three TGs. The inter-rater reliability between the three coders was 86%.

Drawing from the finalized coding scheme from the larger study, in this study, we deeply examined the nature and usage of multimodal representations in one post-CCSS TG. We identified all types of modes (i.e., verbal, actional, and visual modes) showcased through the TG's directives across instructional blocks. Table 2.1 provides the ways the different modes were represented and examples of each mode from the TG.

Subsequently, we examined the patterns in which words were taught by examining the aspects of targeted word knowledge (morphology, semantics, origin, pronunciation, etc.) and modes used during vocabulary-related instruction. Then, we classified instructional blocks in accordance with Paivio and Sadoski's (2001) three scaffold types: representational, referential, and associative. Representational scaffolds of a word occur when non-meaning-based instruction occurs through solely a verbal mode. As suggested by Paivio and Sadoski (2001), familiarity with words at this level may only imply word recognition and does not necessarily signify the ability to define, paraphrase, or give examples. Referential scaffolds are presented when two modes are involved—verbal and non-verbal (e.g., images and gestures)—and the non-verbal mode provides an additional level of meaning to the verbal one. Lastly, an associative scaffold occurs within one mode—verbal or non-verbal—and causes overlapping associations and nested sets between meanings. Guided by these classifications, the first three authors individually identified the types of scaffolds that were recommended to support word knowledge within each instructional block. Afterwards, these individuals compared their classifications, discussed any discrepancies that emerged, and modified the coding process until inter-rater reliability was established. Table 2.2 showcases examples that differentiate the three types of scaffolds.

TABLE 2.1.   Definitions and Examples of Mode Types from the TG

Mode Type	How Modes May be Presented	Example from the TG
Verbal	Pronouncing; sounding out; giving an oral example in a sentence; discussing a word in a context	Draw a three-column chart on the board. In the first column, write non-, un-, dis-, and mis-. In the second column, write violent, friendly, believed, and calculated. Pronounce the prefixes and have students echo-read after you.
Visual	Image; student-made illustrations; text; graphic organizer; movie	Help students use the image on the top of page 45 to understand the meaning of bullying. Have them point to and identify the bullies and their actions. Ask: How does the girl feel? Help students list words that describe bullies and bullying.
Actional	Pantomime; gesture; acting out; pointing to a word	Act out or pantomime the meaning and have students repeat.

TABLE 2.2. Examples of Three Types of Scaffolding

Type of Scaffold	Examples of Grouping	Implemented Modalities
Representational	Remind students that the English language includes words with Latin suffixes. These suffixes provide clues to a word's meaning. The Latin suffixes -ion, -tion, and -ation mean "the act, result, or state of:" They are used to form a noun from a verb: civilization. The Latin suffixes -ty and -ity also mean "the state of:" They are used to form a noun from an adjective: loyalty. The Latin suffixes -fy and -ify mean "to make:' They are used to form a verb: qualify. Point out that this suffix forms a noun from the verb inform. Write the words infection, simplify, and certainty on the board. Have students identify each Latin suffix and then say each word. Review how the suffixes change each base word's part of speech.	*Verbal:* • Initiation of suffixes: does not imply comprehension of the words • Phonological recoding: does not imply understanding the meaning of the words. • Say the word: Does not imply understanding the meaning of the word. *Visual:* • Printed words—does not imply understanding of the word.
Referential	Shades of meaning. Help students generate words and ideas related to generosity. Draw a word web. Label it "generosity." Ask students to reflect on ways that one can show generosity, and any synonyms they can think of. Write down ideas and vocabulary in the web. Add words not included, such as open heart, unselfish. Ask students to copy the words in their word study notebook.	*Visual:* • References between codes that do not have a one-to-one correspondence. • The word generosity can lead to visual referential connections.
Associative	Clarify the meaning. Help students reread the first paragraph on page 37. Define talent, show, juggling, and act. Point to the illustration on page 36 and explain that the girl is juggling in a talent show. Ask: What does Maura want to do in the talent show? Define other difficult words and help students replace the words with words they know.	*Verbal and Non-verbal associations:* • Meaning of word is based on the context: i.e. act; • Verbal code and visual code are associated: • i.e. Juggling and the picture of the girl juggling.

After coding the varying modes (i.e., actional, verbal, and visual) and the three types of scaffolds, we analyzed the patterns that emerged across these different codes.

RESULTS AND DISCUSSION

As suggested by the framework guiding our work, the three types of scaffolds are organized in hierarchical order in terms of promoting deep word learning: representational, referential, and associative. Our coding reveals that the highest frequency of instances (n=9) is among TG directives that promoted associative scaffolding, which suggests the highest level of processing, followed by referential (n=8) and representational (n=6) scaffolding.

Representational Scaffolding

Representational scaffolds recommended in the analyzed TG aim to develop familiarity or recognition of words activated by a linguistic stimulus (a written or oral word) or a nonlinguistic stimulus (an image). The use of representational scaffolding is very consistent across six identified instances in the analyzed TG, when teachers are directed to have students work with words' forms in a graphic organizer.

In the following excerpt, a representational scaffold is used in an instructional block, labeled "Expand Vocabulary," which aims to draw students' attention to different morphological forms of a word and teach them how to use these forms in a sentence:

> Draw a four-column chart on the board. Write advise in the first column. Then write advises, advised, advising in the other three columns. Read aloud the words with students. Have students share sentences using each form of advise. Students can fill in the chart for hesitate and then share sentences using the different forms of the word. Have students copy the chart in their word study notebook.

In the suggested instructional moves, teachers are directed to refer to a T-chart with four columns used to teach inflectional suffixes (-s, -ed, -ing,) of the same root word (advise). Even though this instructional move may potentially increase students' morphological awareness and allow them to use these inflectional endings with other words, these activities do not highlight any semantic information and, thus, do not promote greater depth of knowledge within this activity. More specifically, the exemplar activity shown above does not direct teachers to connect the morphological structure of the word with its meaning, which would help students trace the changes in a word's meanings when transitioning from one form to another.

Referential Scaffolding

Referential scaffolds are between-system connections between the verbal system (words) and in the nonverbal system (images). Our analysis reveals that there are eight instances identified as referential scaffolds in the analyzed units of the TG. Five out of the eight referential scaffolds represent the pattern when a nonlinguistic input (gesture or image) is followed by a target instructional word. The nonlinguistic input includes using illustrations and photographs, pointing to a word, evoking students' imagination, and gestures. The use of gestures is recommended in four out of eight instances of referential scaffolding. The excerpt below is a representative example of referential scaffolding found in an instructional block labeled "Use Visuals:"

> Let's look at the picture for detested. The girl does not like the medicine. She detests it! Model the girl's expression and have students repeat the gesture. Ask: If I

detest something, do I like it or dislike it? Have students complete the frame: Carlos
_____ throwing out the trash. Help students with pronunciation.

In this example, teachers are directed to use three different modes to teach the word "detest:" first showing a picture and simultaneously explaining what it illustrates (the girl who detests medicine). After introducing visual and verbal modes, teachers are suggested to add an actional mode by modeling the gesture of the girl from the picture, and then asking students to repeat the same gesture.

Another instance includes a recommendation to use gestures to point to a light in the room in order to demonstrate the concept of saving energy. Teachers are also directed to provide an explanation that lights use *energy* to subsequently pose a question about how students can save energy in the classroom. No further instruction acknowledging the polysemy of the word *energy* follows, which would offer a greater depth in knowing the word *energy*. It is important to point out that in all types of scaffolding there are suggested directions for introducing more than one vocabulary word to students during the same instructional period. For example, the following words are targeted within one referential type of scaffolding: *advise, desperately, hesitated, humiliated, self-esteem, uncomfortably*. Below is an excerpt showcasing referential scaffolding where usage of vocabulary pictures is followed by a weekly routine:

> Introduce each vocabulary word using the Vocabulary Routine found on the Visual Vocabulary Cards… Have students work with a partner and look at each picture and discuss the definitions of each word. The ask students to choose three words and write questions for their partner to answer using each word.

Referential scaffolding is suggested in this instructional block because target words *advise, desperately, hesitated, humiliated, self-esteem, uncomfortably* are directed to be instructed through the exposure to visual vocabulary cards (through the nonverbal system) combined with the discussion of definitions, writing questions, and answering them in pairs (through the verbal system).

Associative Scaffolding

Associative scaffolds recommended in the analyzed TG aim to develop a network of associations between a word and other word meanings within and across languages in the effort to build a wider semantic network of a word. Notably, associative scaffolds in the TG are primarily used to draw associations between root words and their changes in meaning through the addition of various derivational and inflectional morphemes. It is also important to note that this instruction is intended to take place through the use of graphic organizers in the context of whole-group discussions as shown in the following exemplar of a vocabulary-focused instructional block:

Draw a three-column chart on the board. In the first column, write non, un, dis, and mis. In the second column, write violent, friendly, believed, and calculated. Pronounce the prefixes and have students echo-read after you. Point to the words in the second column and sound them out with students. Have students help you combine the prefixes with the words to create new, longer words: nonviolent, unfriendly, disbelieved, and miscalculated. Write the new words in the third column of the chart and have students choral-read them. Ask students to use the prefixes to help them determine word meanings.

As shown in the previous example, the TG routinely recommends that teachers provide associative scaffolds by displaying words in a graphic organizer that separates words by its morphemes (e.g., root word: violent; affixes: non-, dis-, and mis-). During these tasks, students are expected to associate root words with novel words through interactive discussions that request that they determine word meanings upon adding inflectional (e.g., -s, -ed, -ing) and derivational morphemes (e.g., non, un-, dis-, mis-, -ly, -tion) to root words. Of the associative scaffolds recommended in the TG under analysis, very few of them highlight cross-linguistic associations. Additionally, there are also limited examples that highlight associations between words outside morphological analysis. For instance, we identified very few examples in which highlighting synonyms and antonyms of target words are showcased (e.g., "Draw a synonym/antonym scale. Elicit synonyms and antonyms such as generous, hazardous, unsafe, secure, or harmless. Discuss the meaning of each word and where it should fall on the scale") as recommended instructional moves in the TG.

Summary

Within the representational scaffolds, teachers are primarily suggested to use graphic organizers with multiple morphological forms of the same word. Even though a graphical representation is a type of visual that teachers are recommended to use, there are no directives to include images illustrating the words so that EBs would be able to connect the meaning by hearing/reading a word and simultaneously seeing it on a picture. Within referential scaffolds, teachers are suggested to use different modes—visual, verbal, and actional—when teaching a word. However, there is often a lack of variety in modal usage, when only one mode is suggested for teaching up to 5–7 words in one vocabulary block. Finally, in associative scaffolds provided in the TG, students are frequently expected to associate the root words with the corresponding prefixes and suffixes. Similar to the directives including representational scaffolds, associative scaffolds also direct teachers to primarily focus on the morphological analysis of words.

It is encouraging to see that the post-CCSS TG incorporated all three types of scaffolds (Pavio & Sadoski, 2001), which support EBs' vocabulary development. However, it should be stated that these scaffolds may be better leveraged to promote greater depth of vocabulary knowledge. Namely, the following aspects of word knowledge need to be given more attention through the use of multimodal representations: semantics, polysemy, cognates, denotation/connotation, changes in spelling associated with morphological forms, and pronunciation among others. Moreover, the three types of scaffolds are not used across a variety of modes; the most common pattern observed is using a verbal mode (e.g., saying the word) in tandem with using an image or a gesture. Very few instances within the TG suggest teachers to incorporate multiple modes for instructing target words. Taking into consideration these aspects in the identified usage of multimodal representations, we call teachers for supplemental use of modes. In the following sections, we provide implications for teacher education and classroom strategies for vocabulary instruction.

EXPANDING LITERACY PRACTICES: CLASSROOM STRATEGIES

Based on the findings from this study, we suggest certain classroom strategies to in- and pre-service teachers when supplying multimodal representations of words in efforts to support EBs' vocabulary learning.

Strategy 1: Applying Associative Scaffolds

Our findings indicate that multimodal representations in the analyzed TG are often targeting the morphological aspect of the word knowledge (e.g., work with the prefixes and suffixes as variations of words with the same root). In these activities, teachers are directed to use graphic organizers with separate words, where students are expected to construct new word forms. In this regard, teachers should expand upon the suggested instructional moves in the TGs to promote diverse aspects of word learning, which go beyond morphological awareness. Teachers may modify the suggested activities in ways that make word-learning assignments more meaning-based and context-embedded. Through these modifications, EBs may be better able to explore how words change their meanings when different suffixes are added. Activities showcasing words through multimodal representations can be modified into being meaning-based even when instruction is based on a text, novel situation, or previous experience of EBs.

Strategy 2: Applying Referential Scaffolds

We encourage teachers to use a variety of modes to promote depth of word knowledge. In other words, students should be exposed to different modes that thoroughly represent words. Verbal modes could be recruited through word pronunciation exercises and songs or riddles using the target word. Additionally, visual modes could be employed to showcase written word forms via written text or to depict words through images or video that may also expose EBs to words repeatedly and in a child-friendly manner, which may in turn help to develop a visual concept of the word. Lastly, teachers may also draw from actional modes, linking speech to action, to promote a multi-sensory approach to word learning by requesting or modeling the meaning of a word through physical movement (i.e., gesturing or acting out the meaning of a word).

Strategy 3: Applying Referential Scaffolds

Our study shows that in the analyzed post-CCSS TG, referential scaffolding is used to initially supply a verbal stimulus (word) before associating it with a non-verbal representation, such as pictures. We suggest teachers alternate the mode and provide opportunities for learners to engage with non-verbal representations prior to revealing the target word. With this in mind, activities may become more interactive, enable EBs to activate their background knowledge, and provide greater opportunities to avail themselves of their existing cultural (i.e., drawing from in- and outside-of-school knowledge) and linguistic knowledge (i.e., trans-languaging to convey their knowledge about target words).

Strategy 4: Cross-Applying Referential and Associative Scaffolds

The main format of multimodal representations during vocabulary instruction in the analyzed TG is usage of graphic organizers to instruct morphological aspects of words. There are several instances of using pictures as well as gestures, and no identified examples incorporating videos or alternative sounds (aside from pronouncing the word by the teacher or students, sounding it out or using in a sentence). In this regard, there is a need for diversifying the modes used during the vocabulary instruction, which would also include making cross-linguistic comparisons to highlight how words across languages differ at phonologic, ortho-graphic, semantic, and morphemic levels. For instance, you may display pictures showcasing the meaning of target words to Spanish-speaking students and discuss how cognates in Spanish versus English may appear to be more opaque (e.g., frenesí vs. frenzy) or transparent (e.g., animal vs. animal).

IMPLICATIONS FOR LITERACY TEACHER EDUCATION

As suggested by the existing research, multifaceted instructional approaches support EB's vocabulary development (Carlo et al., 2004; Collins, 2004; Dockrell, Stuard & King, 2010; Nelson, Valdasy, & Sanders, 2011). Recent research indicates that multimodal representations support L2 vocabulary learning and retention and highlights that teaching across multiple modes may be particularly helpful in supporting EB's depth of vocabulary knowledge. The findings of this study indicate that there are different levels of multimodal scaffolding available in the post-CCSS TG. In this regard, we suggest that teacher educators need to inform pre- and in-service teachers about the importance of integrating multiple modes within their vocabulary instruction in order to support EBs.

Additionally, future and current teachers acknowledge that EBs should be af-forded opportunities to navigate between modes during vocabulary learning ac-tivities. Notably, extra-verbal supports used in the classroom are also critical in promoting depth of vocabulary knowledge. In this regard, the following aspects of word knowledge can be targeted during the vocabulary instruction through multimodal representations: morphology, semantics, polysemy, etymology, cognates, and pronunciation among others.

REFLECTION QUESTIONS

1. Which modes do you typically use to represent words to your EB students? Do you employ all available modes to thoroughly represent a word?

2. Are there any difficulties you are faced with when incorporating multimodal representations of words during your work with mainstream students or EB?

3. Reflect on how your classroom routine is set up in terms of using multimodal representations during vocabulary instruction. Are there multiple opportunities to employ multimodal representations of words throughout a lesson? Are the needs of EBs at different levels of proficiency levels met through your vocabulary-related instruction?

4. What strategies could you employ to incorporate EBs' L1 during that also involve using multimodal representations to teach about words?

REFERENCES

August, D. & Shanahan, T. (2006). *Developing literacy in second-language learners: Report of the National Literacy Panel on language-minority children and youth.* Mahwah, NJ: Lawrence Erlbaum Associates.

Avalos, M. A., Malova, I., Massey, S., & Bengochea, A. (2016, April). *Investigating ELs' fourth grade ELA vocabulary instruction pre- and post-CCSS.* Paper presented at American Educational Research Association, Washington, DC.

Bazerman, C. (2006). The writing of social organization and the literate situating of cognition: Extending Goody's Social Implications of Writing. In D. Olson & M. Cole (Eds.), *Technology, literacy and the evolution of society: Implications of the work of Jack Goody* (pp. 215–239). Mahwah, NJ: Erlbaum.

Biemiller, A., & Boote, C. (2006). An effective method for building meaning vocabulary in primary grades. *Journal of Educational Psychology, 98*(1), 44–62.

Bisson, M. J., Heuven, W. J., Conklin, K., & Tunney, R. J. (2014). The role of repeated exposure to multimodal input in incidental acquisition of foreign language vocabulary. *Language Learning, 64*(4), 855–877.

Carlo, M. S., August, D., McLaughlin, B., Snow, C. E., Dressler, C., Lippman, D. N., ... & White, C. E. (2004). Closing the gap: Addressing the vocabulary needs of English-language learners in bilingual and mainstream classrooms. *Reading Research Quarterly, 39,* 188–215.

Carpenter, S., & Olson, K. (2012). Are pictures good for learning new vocabulary in a foreign language? Only if you think they are not. *Journal of Experimental Psychology: Learning, Memory, and Cognition, 38*(1), 92–101.

Clark, J. M., & Paivio, A. (1991). Dual coding theory and education. *Educational Psychology Review, 3*(3), 149–170.

Collins, M. F. (2004). ESL preschoolers' English vocabulary acquisition from storybook reading. *Early Childhood Research Quarterly, 25*, 84–97.

Dockrell, J. E., Stuart, M., & King, D. (2010). Supporting early oral language skills for English language learners in inner city preschool provision. *British Journal of Educational Psychology, 80*(4), 497–515.

Dubois, M. & Vial, I. (2000). Multimedia design: the effects of relating multimodal information. *Journal of Computer Assisted Learning, 16*, 157–165.

Echevarria, J., Vogt, M. E. & Short, D. (2013). *Making content comprehensible for English learners: The SIOP Model,* (4th Ed.) Boston, MA: Allyn & Bacon.

García, O. (1983). Sociolinguistics and language planning in bilingual education for Hispanics in the United States. *International Journal of the Sociology of Language, 44*, 43–54.

García, O. (2009). Encountering indigenous bilingualism. *Journal of Language, Identity,and Education, 8*(5), 376–380.

García, O., Kleifgen, J., & Falchi, L. (2008). *From English language learners to emergent bilinguals.* New York, NY: Campaign for Educational Equity, Teachers College, Columbia University.

Gersten, R., & Baker, S. (2000). Effective instruction for English language learners: What we know about effective instructional practices for English language learners. *Exceptional Children, 66*(4), 454–470.

Gersten, R., & Geva, E. (2003). Teaching reading to early language learners. *Educational Leadership, 60*(7), 44–49.

Graves, M., August, D., & Mancilla-Martinez, J. (2012). *Teaching vocabulary to English language learners.* New York, NY: Teachers College Press.

Hargrave, A., & Sénéchal, M. (2000). A book reading intervention with preschool children who have limited vocabularies: The benefits of regular reading and dialogic reading. *Early Childhood Research Quarterly,15*, 75–90.

Howard, E. R., Sugarman, J., & Coburn, C. (2006). *Adapting the Sheltered Instruction Observation Protocol (SIOP) for Two-Way Immersion Education: An Introduction to the TWIOP.* Washington, DC: Center for Applied Linguistics.

Kost, C. R., Foss P., & Lenzini J. (1999). Textual and pictorial glosses: Effectiveness on incidental vocabulary growth when reading in a foreign language. *Foreign Language Annals, 32*, 89–113.

Lugo-Neris, M. J., Jackson, C. & Goldstein, H. (2010). Facilitating vocabulary acquisition of young English language learners. *Speech and Hearing Services in Schools, 41*, 314–327.

Marulis, L. M. & Neuman, S. B. (2010). The effects of vocabulary intervention on young children's word learning: A Meta-Analysis. *Review of Educational Research, 80*, 300–335.

Moats, L. C. (2001). Overcoming the language gap. *American Educator, 25*(5), 8–9.

Nation, I. S. P. (2013). *Learning vocabulary in another language* (2nd ed.). New York, NY: Cambridge University Press.

National Governor's Association Center for Best Practices & Council of Chief State School Officers. (2010a). *Common core state standards for English language arts.* Washington, DC: Authors. Retrieved from http://www.corestandards.org/ELA-Literacy

National Reading Panel (2000). *Teaching children to read: An evidence-based assessment of the scientific research literature on reading and its implications for reading instruction.* Washington, DC: U. S. Department of Health and Human Services.

Norris, S. (2004). *Analyzing multimodal interaction: A methodological framework.* New York, NY: Routledge.

Nelson, J. R., Valdas, P. F., & Sanders, E. A., (2011). Efficacy of a Tier 2 supplemental root word vocabulary and decoding intervention with kindergarten Spanish-speaking, English learners. *Journal of Literacy Research, 43*(2), 184–211.

Paivio, A., & Sadoski, M. (2001). *Imagery and text: A dual coding theory of reading and writing.* Mahwah, NJ: Lawrence Erlbaum Associates.

Paivio, A., & Sadoski, M. (2011). Lexicons, contexts, events, and images: Commentary on Elman (2009) from the perspective of Dual Coding Theory. *Cognitive Science, 35*, 198–209.

Plass, J., Chun, D. M., Mayer, R. & Leutner, D. (1998). Supporting visual and verbal learning preferences in a second language multimedia learning environment. *Journal of Educational Psychology, 90*, 25–36.

Proctor, C. P., Uccelli, P., Dalton, B., & Snow, C. E. (2009). Understanding depth of vocabulary online with bilingual and monolingual children. *Reading & Writing Quarterly, 25*(4), 311–333.

Reyes, I. (2006). Exploring connections between emergent biliteracy and bilingualism. *Journal of Early Childhood Literacy, 6*(3), 267–292.

Royce, T. (2002). Multimodality in the TESOL classroom: Exploring visual-verbal synergy. *TESOL Quarterly, 36*(2), 191–205.

Sadoski M. & Paivio, A. (2001) *Imagery and text: A dual coding theory of reading and writing.* Mahwah, NJ: Lawrence Erlbaum Associates Publishers.

Sadoski, M., & Paivio, A. (2004). A dual coding theoretical model of reading. *Theoretical models and processes of reading, 5*, 1329–1362.

Silverman, R. D. (2007). Vocabulary development of English-language and English-only learners in kindergarten. *The Elementary School Journal, 107*(4), 365–383.

Ulanoff, S. H., & Pucci, S.L. (1999). Learning words from books: The effects of read aloud on second language vocabulary acquisition. *Bilingual Research Journal, 23*(4), 409–422.

CHAPTER 3

USING MULTIMODAL PRACTICES TO SUPPORT STUDENTS' ACCESS TO ACADEMIC LANGUAGE AND CONTENT IN SPANISH AND ENGLISH

Sabrina F. Sembiante, J. Andrés Ramírez, and Luciana C. de Oliveira

This chapter considers the potential for expanding literacy practices to include multimodal literacy for emergent-to-advanced bilingual (EAB) students in dual language programs. We showcase how teachers can apply a multimodal literacy approach in their teaching to support students' access to academic language and content in Spanish and English texts. We consider the purposes of the images and texts in U.S. English and Spanish-language textbooks and the manner in which they can be utilized to develop students' bilingual academic content knowledge and language in the content areas.

Expanding Literacy Practices Across Multiple Modes and
Languages for Multilingual Students, pages 39–55.

Literacy entails making sense of written symbols whose meaning is created and derived from social practices (Barton, 1994). In order to become literate in society, students must navigate the social context in which the text is found, the text's purpose, and what they bring to the text, such as their own background, language, and literacy experiences (Walsh, 2010). Multimodal literacy honors this complexity and adds to it by acknowledging the many ways that knowledge is represented and deployed in texts through different modalities (e.g., image, words, sound, and movement) (Jewitt & Kress, 2003). To adequately make meaning of texts and social contexts in which a range of modalities is used to communicate information, students must become competent users and producers of multimodal texts themselves, understanding how each modality contributes separately and simultaneously to construct meaning (Walsh, 2008).

For emergent-to-advanced bilingual (EAB) students, who are learning more than one language and who negotiate more than one culture (García, 2009), their biliteracy and multimodal literacy development is potentially more complex because each develops in reference to their multiple languages and cultural contexts. In dual language programs that provide formal bilingual academic language and literacy instruction, multimodal literacy can be incorporated in an effort to enhance students' ability for meaning-making across modalities, languages, and literacies. In this chapter, we consider the potential for expanding literacy practices to include multimodal literacy for EAB students in dual language programs. We highlight how teachers can facilitate students' access to the academic content and language of English and Spanish textbooks through multimodal practices.

ACADEMIC LANGUAGE DEVELOPMENT FOR EMERGENT TO ADVANCED BILINGUAL STUDENTS

If students are to perform successfully in academic contexts, they need to be provided with opportunities to develop the language of schooling (Schleppegrell, 2004). Since EAB students learn through language and about language in schools (Halliday, 1993), researchers and practitioners have directed special attention to the kind of language that these students need for school success (see, for example, de Oliveira, Sembiante, & Ramirez, 2018). This language, commonly called *academic language*, is defined as the lexical, grammatical, and discourse features of written and oral language used in instructional or text-based interactions within the content areas (Bailey & Butler, 2003). Similar to Alvarez's (2012) expansion of the academic language term, we use this term to account for the varying functions and uses of academic language across different genres of text. Although discussion persists about how to best support and facilitate EAB students' academic language development in school contexts, considerations have failed to address the "types and range of experiences and interactions that must surround minority youngsters if they are to acquire the kinds of language proficiencies considered desirable by educational institutions" (Valdés, 2010).

The discrepancy between EAB students' informal and formal oracy and literacy skills have been made clear and can be traced back to Skutnabb-Kangas and Toukomaa's (1976) study documenting this phenomenon. Finnish immigrant children in Sweden frequently appeared to educators as conversationally fluent in both Finnish and Swedish but with levels of academic performance in both languages that were considerably below grade and age expectations. This distinction between verbal and academic performance was later theorized within the common underlying proficiency theory by Jim Cummins (1979). Cummins distinguished between basic interpersonal communicative skills (BICS) or conversational fluency and cognitive academic language proficiency (CALP) or academic language proficiency. During the 1980s and 90s, the BICS and CALP classification served as catalyst to distinguish playground language from classroom language (Gibbons, 1991). With vivid and engaging examples from these settings, Gibbons highlights the particular demands and linguistic challenges of classroom language.

As discussion on the meaning of academic language continued, other researchers pointed to the fact that, ironically for the digital age, the discussion has been overwhelmingly monomodal (i.e., focused on only one mode) and graphocentric (i.e., focused on only text) (Block, 2013). This left other semiotic, or meaning-making, aspects like accompanying images undertheorized (The New London Group, 1996). Language use today arises in part from the characteristics of digital information and communications media. Meaning is made in ways that are increasingly multimodal as linguistic modes of meaning interface with oral, visual, audio, gestural, tactile, and spatial resources for communication (Kress & Van Leeuwen, 2001).

These advances in language and literacy have important and complex implications for the classroom. Teachers' sole focus on language when working with textbooks and, consequently, with their literacy pedagogy, needs to be expanded to encompass the full range of semiotic resources so that the privileging of alphabetical representations does not persist. Contemporary communication tools now available to publishing companies have increased the complexity of academic texts such that they are multigeneric and multimodal, with digital technologies seamlessly integrated within existing curriculum and assessment (Jewitt, 2002). Unfortunately, the increased attention and theorization of the conversational/academic language distinction by researchers still needs to be translated into teachers' practice.

While some scholars have attempted to provide teachers with techniques that shelter academic content and language for EAB students, these strategies often simplify the content and language to the point of changing the material or diminishing the necessary academic concepts (e.g., Echevarria, Vogt, & Short, 2007).

One key illustration of this lack of correspondence is the fact that many studies have pointed out to teachers' understanding of academic language as mainly concerned with technical, content area vocabulary, or "hard words" (Gottlieb & Ernst-Slavit, 2014, p. 4). This simplification of academic language has been common and widespread among teachers and it is indicative of the breach between theory and practice. The recent arrival of the Common Core State Standards has brought a renewed interest and concern with academic language from teachers who slowly but surely are coming to the realization that academic language entails much more than technical vocabulary related to a specific content area (de Oliveira, 2012).

Textbooks are a central "pedagogic device" (Bernstein, 1996) in classrooms, a primary way in which curricula are planned and deployed, and a principal source of academic language and content for students (Apple, 2008; de Oliveira, Sembiante, & Ramirez, 2018). When considering the modalities employed to communicate this information, we note that contemporary textbooks contain a myriad of images that combine with text to facilitate the books' clearly defined and pedagogical objectives (Bezemer & Kress, 2008). By only focusing on text, we are hindering the meaning-making potential of students and their access to the information available in the text. Taking on a multimodal literacy approach is an important step in expanding the literacy practices of teachers and students. While we acknowledge the potential of multimodality-driven instructional practices, more investigation and practical techniques must be provided in order for this approach to be realized pedagogically (Walsh, 2009). In this chapter, we showcase how teachers can apply a multimodal literacy approach in their teaching to support students' access to academic language and content in Spanish and English texts. We are guided by the following two questions:

1. What are the purposes of the images and texts in U.S. English and Spanish-language textbooks?
2. How can they be utilized to develop students' bilingual academic content knowledge and language in the content areas?

METHODOLOGY

This study focuses on an analysis of the visual and verbal modes (i.e., images and text) in English and Spanish textbooks. By determining why and how images and text are included in textbooks, teachers are afforded ways to engage students in the multimodal aspects that support their development of academic content knowledge and language.

Data Collection

Our data includes a corpus of language arts, science, social studies, and mathematics textbooks published by McMillan, McGraw-Hill, and Houghton-Mifflin in English and Spanish. These textbooks are currently being used with EAB students in dual language programs in the Broward and Palm Beach school districts in Florida. The English and Spanish textbooks are mirrored texts, meaning that the content in English has been translated to Spanish for the Spanish-language textbook and each version of the book contains the same images and meaning of text on each page. Although the manner in which EAB students are directed to use these textbooks varies within and across dual language programs, students are often using either the English or Spanish textbook for different subject areas, meaning that they are required to access the content of the text through a language they may still be learning.

Data Analysis

Textbooks used in K–12 classrooms are rarely constructed solely of text. Instead, they feature many different types of images, graphs, tables, figures, and other visual modes that reinforce, compete with, and contextualize the text to construct meaning (Nodelman, 1988). We use Painter, Martin, and Unsworth's (2013) framework for image analysis to reveal the meanings of a textbook created through the intermodal use of image and text. This framework, based upon Halliday's (1978) systemic functional linguistics, guides us to consider three questions:

1. What content or subject matter is being expressed by the image and the text?
2. How is the image or text communicating with the reader? What are the roles and relationships between the image/text and reader?
3. How is the image and text organized and relevant in relation to other images/texts and the larger context?

By applying this framework, we are able to gain further insight into the broader system of signs and symbols (i.e., the social semiotic system) that are employed to make meaning in textbooks (Painter, Marin, & Unsworth, 2013). In our results section below, we present the framework and provide examples of how it can be applied to expose additional layers of meaning available in the textbook. We encourage teachers to employ this framework and identify the intermodal meanings of image and text in the textbooks they work with. In turn, this knowledge can inform their instruction of EAB students and help them to teach their students how to recognize and make sense of these meanings for themselves, providing them with additional access to the academic content and language of the textbook.

TABLE 3.1.   Framework for Analyzing Images and Texts: Guiding Questions, and Image and Language Demands

Guiding Questions	Image Demands to Identify	Language Demands to Identify
1. What content or subject matter is being expressed by the image and the text?	**Character manifestation** (salient features of character appearance that are repeated) **Character appearance** (first and reappearance of character & inference of "same/changed identity")	**Participants**
	Processes (depicting an event or action carried out by a participant)	**Processes** (verbs)
	Circumstances (the physical environment/ spatial location in which the characters act)	**Circumstances** (prepositional phrases)
2. How is the image or text communicating with the reader? What are the roles and relationships between the image/text and reader?	**Focalization** (whether the viewer has been positioned to engage with the character via eye contact or to observe the depicted participant)	**Mood** (statements, commands, questions)
	Graduation (ways of upscaling or downscaling evaluative meanings or attitudinal impact of visual elements; through high number or same item, large scale relative to other comparable elements, or the item taking up large amounts of available space)	
	Affect (particular ways of presenting a character's emotions through facial features and bodily stance)	**Modality** (modal verbs and adverbial phrases)
	Pathos (the degree of detail and realism of drawing; appreciative, empathic, personalizing)	
	Ambience (the emotional effect of the use of color on viewer)	
3. How is the image and text organized and relevant in relation to other images/texts and the larger context?	**Layout** (whether verbiage is integrated, incorporated as part of visual image, or is complementary, placed in distinct spaces within layout—weight/Importance based on amount of visual space being taken up; new/given)	**Theme/Rheme** (Theme = first elements of each clause up to the process Rheme = the rest of the clause including the process)
	Framing (framed or if it extends whole page)	
	Focus (visual elements placed in a compositional relation so as to be apprehended at a glance; if complementary, we will attend to its parts separately and respond to any image within the layout as an additional focus group in its own right)	**Reference** (referential pronouns; nominalizations)

RESULTS

In this section, we use examples to showcase how to implement the framework for analyzing images and texts. The framework guides us to consider the multiple modes of the text and how they create meaning. Specifically, our analysis is driven by the three guiding questions in our framework: (a) What content or subject matter is being expressed by the image and the text? (b) How is the image or text communicating with the reader and what are the roles and relationships constructed between image, text, and reader? (c) How is the image and text organized and relevant in relation to other images/texts and the larger context? We have organized this section according to our findings for each question and discuss the results of our analysis by first addressing text and then images for each specific demand. We have chosen to present our findings through analysis of one page of a 3rd grade Science textbook in English and in Spanish. This page is the initial introduction in a unit entitled "How do scientists investigate questions?" This unit also represented the first unit of the Science textbook and the first content that students would encounter if working from the beginning of the textbook.

Subject Matter Expressed by the Image and Text

The guiding question "What content or subject matter is being expressed by the image and the text?" asks that we recognize the ways that text and image

FIGURE 3.1.   English and Spanish Textbook Excerpts

express the primary participants (i.e., characters), processes (i.e., actions), and circumstantial information of the subject matter. By distinguishing what these are in the text and image, students can connect this information across modes to bolster their understanding of the text. We combine the analysis of text and image to show how they are related.

Participants, Character Manifestation and Appearance. When identifying these features in the text of the page, we look for the participants, expressed through nouns, used in the text. This helps us and our students to understand who or what the text is about. For our sample textbook page, we see that the participants are: *scientists/científicos, questions/preguntas, your brain, the answer/la repuesta, the following question/la siguiente pregunta, this lesson/esta lección, this student/este estudiante, a scientist/un científico, active Reading/lectura, un propósito, lesson vocabulary/vocabulario, una lista, each term/los términos, notes/notas, the interactive glossary/el Glosario interactivo, headings/títulos, active readers/los buenos lectores, the headings/los títulos, Headings/Los titulos, the reader/al lector, an idea/una idea, the reading/la lectura, a purpose/un propósito, active readers/los lectores*. We can see that many of these participants are representative of constituents of a classroom (e.g., scientists, student, lesson, readers) and of a lesson (e.g., answer, question, reading, vocabulary, glossary).

When identifying who or what the image is about, we look at the character's appearance and how the character is manifested in the picture. When can see that the salient features of the character's appearance include the boy, whose face is partly shown, and who is masked by a butterfly that he is holding with his finger. The butterfly is shown so closely that the reader can see details of its wing. If one were to flip through a few pages of the textbook, you notice that the first and last appearance of the boy and the butterfly is on this page, telling us that the significance of their appearance is in the way they are shown here. Thus, teachers can help students to understand that the boy in the picture represents a scientist. An analysis of participants also helps teachers and students to be aware that while the images link to the topic of investigation, the rest of the text discusses the function and use of headings, which the teacher and students would need to look for explicitly.

Processes. To identify the processes in the text, we find the verbs in every sentence that communicate to us the actions or relationships taking place. From the sample textbook page, we find the following processes: *do investigate/investigan, responder, engage/ponte a pensar, find/halla, record/escribela, is acting/está actuando, list/haz (una lista), learn/aprendes, make notes/toma notas, preview or read/dan (un vistazo), give/dan, is/trata, reading/leer, helps/ayuda, understand/entender, are reading/leen*. Many of these verbs represent mental processes (e.g., investigate, engage, think/pensar, learn, read) that would be expected of a student in a classroom engaged in a lesson.

To identify the processes represented in the image, we ask ourselves what event or action the characters or participants are depicted carrying out in the image. We notice that there is no physical action that is portrayed in the picture, but the boy is standing and holding the butterfly in a way that shows he is looking at the butterfly, and possibly, thinking about it. Thus, the action being depicted in the picture seems to revolve around perceiving and considering the object under study, the butterfly. Here, students who have been taught to connect their knowledge of language and visual modes will be able to make the connection that the boy's observation of the butterfly represents the action of investigating. Connections such as these have the potential to bolster students' understanding of the purpose and language of the content area text.

Circumstances. To identify the circumstances of the text, teachers must look for prepositional phrases (i.e., phrases beginning with prepositions like *in, for, to, about, of*) that provide additional information about when, where, how, and why. When analyzing the text for these phrases, we find examples such as: *to the following question/ a la siguiente pregunta, in this lesson/en esta lección, here/aquí, con propósito, about each/cada uno, in the interactive glossary/en el Glosario interactivo, of what the reading is about/ de lo que trata la lectura, with a purpose/ con un propósito.* We notice that these phrases inform us of the matter (e.g., Find the answer *to the following question* in this lesson), the location (e.g., Find the answer to the following question *in this lesson*), and accompaniment (e.g., Reading *with a purpose* helps…), among other circumstances. This helps teachers and students contextualize the participants (nouns) and processes (verbs).

When considering details of the circumstance provided in the image, teachers should push their students to consider the aspects of the physical environment or the spatial location provided in which the character or participants interact. In the sample textbook page, we notice that the boy and the butterfly are located outside since there is foliage in the background of the picture. The boy seems to have found a butterfly and is examining it in its natural habitat. By noticing where the boy is, what he is doing, and how he is holding the butterfly—all details provided by the physical environment/spatial location—students are able to place the participants in a context and better understand their related purposes.

Roles and Relationships between the Image, Text, and Reader

The guiding questions "How is the image or text communicating with the reader? What are the roles and relationships between the image/text and reader?" ask that we recognize the ways that text, image, and reader are positioned interpersonally with one another. To identify the nature of the text-image and text-reader relationships, we consider the mood of sentences (i.e., if statements, questions, or commands are being used) and the use of modal verbs (i.e., should, could, will, would, may, and other words that indicate different levels of probability, usuality, willingness, and obligation) in the text. Conversely, to learn about the image-text and image-reader relationships, we consider the focal aspects of the image (focalization), the emotions presented (affect), the realistic nature in which the characters are portrayed (pathos), the effect of color on emotional and interpersonal impact (ambience), and the scaling of elements in the image (graduation).

Mood, Focalization and Graduation. When considering the mood of text, a teacher can ascertain the purpose of the text based on whether sentences are in the form of statements that provide information, questions that ask students to find an appropriate response, or commands that tell students to act or think in a particular way. Identifying these aspects in the example text page, we notice that there are only two open-ended questions (e.g., *how do scientists investigate questions?/¿cómo investigan los científicos para responder preguntas?, how is this student acting like a scientist?/Por qué está estudiante actuando como un cientifico?*) asking students to think about particular content and find appropriate answers. There are three statements (e.g., *active readers preview.../los Buenos lectores dan..., headings give.../los titulus le dan..., Reading with a purpose helps.../Leer con un proposito ayuda...*) providing factual information for students. Lastly, there are four commands (e.g., *engage your brain, find the answers.../halla la respuesta..., record it here/excribela aguí, list each term.../haz una lista..., make notes.../toma notas...*) telling students what to do and how to act in response to the text. Based on this analysis, we can see that the purpose of the text is mostly to command students to act in particular ways that have been identified to elicit learning (finding answers, taking notes, recording, and listing). When taking a closer look at the commands, the teacher can help students to notice that the commands tell students what to do with the information that they generate from the questions.

To identify focalization, or ways that readers have been positioned to engage with the characters or participants in the image, we consider how we are made to observe or engage with the picture. In terms of graduation, we also consider which elements in the image are scaled up or down in the image to impact the viewer. In our sample textbook page, we notice that we are positioned as an observer of the boy who is holding the butterfly. However, we also can see that the boy is holding out the butterfly for us, the observers, to perceive closely. The butterfly has been scaled up relative to the other elements in the picture so that the obvious focus is on the butterfly. This seems to be done purposefully since the butterfly would be smaller than the boy holding it. Thus, the focal aspects of the image seem to be the butterfly over the boy, since the boy's face is partly hidden and unfocused and the detail of butterfly's wings is clearly distinguished to attract attention. When connecting this information to the text, we understand that there is a supportive link between the questions being asked and the design of the image. Students can use the image as a cognitive support when responding to the cognitively-challenging, inferential questions. The text-image link is one that teachers could purposefully highlight and emphasize for EAB students in support of their academic language learning.

Modality, Affect, Pathos, and Ambience. The use of modal verbs in the text helps us to consider the degree of negativity/positivity as well as the judgment being made on the content or of the reader. When analyzing the sample textbook page, we notice that there are no modal verbs used (e.g., may, might, will, should, much, could, can) and thus, there is no nuance on the information that communicates different degrees of probability, usuality, willingness, and obligation. Thus, the facts provided, the requests being asked, and the commands requiring action represent fixed information that students are not being asked to consider in tempered ways.

When considering affect in an image, teachers must look at how characters' emotions are presented through facial features and bodily stance. Pathos guides us to analyze how realistically characters' faces and bodies are depicted while ambience asks viewers to reflect upon the effect of color in the image. Together, these visual modes help the viewer to consider ways in which they are being asked to feel or respond to the image, as well as the degree of negativity/positivity reflected in the picture. We notice that the boy is smiling behind the butterfly, and seems to be content with the situation. Both participants are depicted realistically in the picture given that this is an actual photograph. The facial features of the boy are not very distinct since he is situated in the background. Although he is looking at the camera, his head and body angle are tilted sideways and only a portion of his face is visible. The butterfly is seen in profile and is shown close up so that the details of its wings are evident. In terms of color, green takes up most of the page. The butterfly is shown in brown but the markings on the wings are light and contrast well with the brown of the wing. The titles and headings in the areas of text are written in contrasting colors (light blue and yellow) than the colors of the background. Areas for writing activities are in white which also contrast highly with the image in the background. By taking affect, pathos, and ambience, we note that the image is communicating to us the centrality of the butterfly in the large background picture, as well as the importance of the bolded headings, since they are contrasted so clearly with one another. This implicitly relates to the content and purpose of the questions (to have students make inferences) as opposed to the content and purpose of the commands (to have students engage in learning tasks as delineated by headings). Thus, by having teachers instruct students on how to "read the image", students can render support and connections with the text, facilitating their learning and understanding of academic language.

Organization of Image and Text and their Relationship to Larger Context

The guiding question "How is the image and text organized and relevant in relation to other images/texts and the larger context?" helps us consider how the organization of modes builds meaning in the text. With regard to the text, we identify the information provided in the theme, or subject of each sentence, and the rheme, or the predicate of the sentence to see how new and given information is structured and ordered. We also identify any references in the text that create connection and cohesiveness across sentences and paragraphs. In terms of the image, we consider the layout (i.e., where text is placed in contrast to the image), framing (i.e., how expansive the image is on the page), and focus (i.e., the composition of visual elements) to gain further insight into the text.

Theme-Rheme, Layout and Framing. By looking at the Theme or the point of departure of each sentence related to the paragraph entitled "Use Headings/Usa los titulus", we notice that the Themes of these sentences are "*active readers/los buenos lectores, headings/los titulos, reading with a purpose/leer con propósito*" while the Rheme of these sentences serves to provide information about that participant. We also note that the information provided in the Rheme of one sentence (e.g., Active readers preview, or read, *the headings* first), appears as the Theme in the subsequent sentence (e.g., *Headings* give the reader an idea of...), showing how the text organizes new and given information to develop content knowledge.

To analyze the layout of the image for the meaning it contributes to the text, we look for how verbiage is integrated within the image and we use its placement as an indication of its importance in relation to the picture. The text seems to occupy the largest portion of the page and is complementary to the picture, placed in a distinct space within the layout rather than integrated or incorporated as part of the image. Since the text and prompts take up most of the space on the page, importance seems to be given to text in lieu of the picture, which plays a secondary, more supportive role. In terms of framing, the writing and prompts are either framed in contrast to the dark background or specifically with a yellow border, again suggesting text to be the priority on this page. The background picture extends the whole page, probably to provide adequate room for the text to take up a central position.

Reference and Focus. When considering how references contribute to the organization and coherence of the text, we recognize several that help to tie information together. For example, the text states "Find the answer to the following question in this lesson and record it here". The term "the answer" and "it" is a reference to the question first asked of students, while "this lesson" indirectly references the textbook page and specifies its purpose as a lesson. The phrase "How is this student acting like a scientist?" also contains references that are important for students to understand, such as "this student" which speaks directly to the boy portrayed in the picture, and "like a scientist" which is a reference back to the student, specifying his role in the picture. These references are the most explicit way in which the text connects itself to the image. Understanding these connections will allow students to use the visual modes as a support for their understanding of the academic language.

The last aspect of organization that we can attend to in the image is its focus, or where parts of the image are placed in relation to each other. We notice that the main image in the sample textbook page is not made up of separate parts, and instead is meant to be viewed and understood as a cohesive image. There is one separate image of a small cartoon drawing of a brain that is not connected to the boy and butterfly, and is placed as a support and reference to the heading "Engage your Brain". The heading itself is written on a banner that ends with an arrow, indicating to the viewer that the command is intended to relate to the picture. The background photo is designed to be viewed first, serving a contextualizing role for the student as they begin to read. Conversely, the students are meant to encounter the cartoon brain as they go from reading the question to reading the prompt "Engage your Brain" since it is drawn in front of and in line with the text.

By encouraging students to connect verbal and visual modalities, teachers can help their EAB students gain additional access to the English or Spanish academic language of the textbook. EAB students who are taught to recruit and apply their range of multimodal resources will be able to connect the linguistic features of the text with their visual counterparts in the image and develop a more nuanced, profound understanding of the academic language.

DISCUSSION AND IMPLICATIONS FOR LITERACY TEACHER EDUCATION

Our analyses of the textbook pages revealed that the interrelationship of text and image on a page is systematic and contains many clues, reinforcements, and extensions of the text. In lieu of providing images as a shallow type of support for EAB students, as has been suggested in the past recommendations for instruction (e.g., Echevarria, Vogt, & Short, 2007), our framework encourages teachers and students to unlock the meaning that is indexed by the content, relationship, and organization of text and image in very linguistically and visually explicit ways. As EAB students have been encouraged to do with their rich repertoire of language, our framework provides a way that teachers can have students apply their multimodal resources to decode and learn the blueprint of language.

In their biliteracy development, EAB students may learn literacy skills through either language and apply that knowledge across their languages (Brisk & Harrington, 2010). Just as their literacy learning in one language supports that of another, EAB students come to the task of developing academic content and language with a rich language repertoire and an advanced awareness of the meaning-making resources that can be employed across languages. Multimodal literacy builds upon EAB students' prior cross-linguistic understandings and asks students to consider and combine the meaning potential of images with their current bilingual and biliterate sense-making processes. By adhering to the framework presented above, students can be taught to look for salient aspects in the image (e.g., character appearance, color and ambience, foregrounded/backgrounded picture elements) and seek their connection to portions of text to gain a deeper understanding of academic language and the academic content it indexes.

Thinking about the image in these ways will also help revolutionize how EAB students may consider the text. They may come to understand that just as the image communicates subject matter, dictates roles and relationships with the text and reader, and is purposefully organized, these aspects exist in text too. By learning about image and text in this way, EAB students are not approaching academic

TABLE 3.2. Framework for Analyzing Images and Texts: Guiding Questions, Image and Language Demands, and Tasks for Teachers

Guiding Questions	Image Demands to Identify	Language Demands to Identify	Tasks for Teachers to Perform
1. What content or subject matter is being expressed by the image and the text?	**Character manifestation** (salient features of character appearance that are repeated) **Character appearance** (first and reappearance of character & inference of "same/changed identity") **Process** (depicting an event or action carried out by a participant) **Circumstance** (the physical environment/spatial location in which the characters act)	**Participants** **Processes** (verbs) **Circumstances** (prepositional phrases)	Identify the content or subject matter being conveyed by the text or image.
2. How is the image or text communicating with the reader? What are the roles and relationships between the image/text and reader?	**Focalization** (whether the viewer has been positioned to engage with the character via eye contact or to observe the depicted participant) **Graduation** (ways of upscaling or downscaling evaluative meanings or attitudinal impact of visual elements; through high number or same item, large scale relative to other comparable elements, or the item taking up large amounts of available space) **Affect** (particular ways of presenting a character's emotions through facial features and bodily stance) **Pathos** (the degree of detail and realism of drawing; appreciative, empathic, personalizing) **Ambience** (the emotional effect of the use of color on viewer)	**Mood** (statements, commands, questions) **Modality** (modal verbs and adverbial phrases)	Identify the relationship set up between the image, the text, and the reader.
3. How is the image and text organized and relevant in relation to other images/texts and the larger context?	**Layout** (whether verbiage is integrated, incorporated as part of visual image, or is complementary, placed in distinct spaces within layout—weight/importance based on amount of visual space being taken up; new/given) **Framing** (framed or if it extends whole page) **Focus** (visual elements placed in a compositional relation so as to be apprehended at a glance; if complementary, we will attend to its parts separately and respond to any image within the layout as an additional focus group in its own right)	**Theme/Rheme** (Theme = first elements of each clause up to the process; Rheme = the rest of the clause including the process) **Reference** (referential pronouns; nominalizations)	Identify the connection and organization of text to image.

language learning in a piecemeal manner, but are accessing the very blueprint of the semiotic system in its entirety. This communicates to students that academic language is much more than just the learning of discipline-specific vocabulary, requiring an intimate knowledge of particular grammatical and rhetorical conventions that shift across content areas (Schleppegrell, 2004). The three guiding questions in the framework provide a concrete way for teachers to help their EAB students gain entry into academic language and its content, and it does so by harnessing students' own rich multimodal and multilingual expertise.

EXPANDING LITERACY PRACTICES: CLASSROOM STRATEGIES

Strategy 1: Determining Why and How Images and Text are Included in Textbooks

The framework we provide in this chapter helps teachers to reveal the meanings through the intermodal use of image and text. We added "tasks for teachers to perform" to help teachers analyze the text and image. Our analysis above can also serve as a model for teacher analysis.

Strategy 2: Engaging students in the multimodal aspects of text

Teachers can provide students with opportunities to engage with the multimodal aspects of text by exploring some aspects of the analysis that teachers conduct using the table presented under strategy 1. Multimodal instruction makes content knowledge more vivid for learners and is especially beneficial for EAB students. Teachers can explore the images by asking three simple questions: 1. What is going on in this image? 2. What makes you say that? 3. What is the relationship between what is presented in the image and what is presented in the text?

REFLECTION QUESTIONS
(INCLUDE 4–5 REFLECTION QUESTIONS)

1. How do the ideas about expanding literacy practices included in this chapter apply to your teaching context?
2. How do you plan to incorporate multimodal literacy for EAB students and all of the students in your classroom?
3. What aspects of the multimodal analysis presented here are most relevant?
4. What areas do you feel you need to learn more about related to multimodal literacy?

REFERENCES

Alvarez, L. (2012). Reconsidering academic language in practice: The demands of Spanish expository reading and students' bilingual resources. *Bilingual Research Journal,* *35*(1), 32–52.

Apple, M. W. (2008). Curriculum planning: Content, form and politics of accountability. In F. M. Connelly, M. Fang He, & J. Phillion (Eds.), *The SAGE handbook of curriculum and instruction* (pp. 25–44). Thousand Oaks, CA: Sage Publications, Inc.

Bailey, A. L., & Butler, F. A. (2003). *An evidentiary framework for operationalizing academic language for broad application to K–12 education: A design document. CSE report.* Washington, DC: Institute of Education Sciences. (ERIC Document Reproduction Service No. ED483026).

Barton, D. (1994). *Literacy: An introduction to the ecology of written language.* London, UK: Blackwell.

Bernstein, B. (1996). *Pedagogy, symbolic control & identity theory.* London, UK: Taylor and Francis.

Bezemer, J., & Kress, G. (2008). Writing in multimodal texts: A social semiotic account of designs for learning. *Written Communication, 25*(2), 166–195.

Block, D. (2013). Moving beyond "lingualism": Multilingual embodiment and multimodality in SLA. In S. May (Ed.), *The multilingual turn: Implications for SLA, TESOL and bilingual education* (pp. 54–77). New York, NY: Routledge.

Brisk, M. E., & Harrington, M. M. (2010). *Literacy and bilingualism: A handbook for all teachers.* New York, NY: Routledge.

Cummins, J. (1979). Linguistic interdependence and the educational development of bilingual children. *Review of Educational Research, 49*(2), 222–259.

de Oliveira, L. C. (2012). What history teachers need to know about academic language to teach English language learners. *The Social Studies Review, 51*(1), 76–79.

de Oliveira, L. C., Sembiante, S., & Ramirez, J. A. (2018). Bilingual academic language development in mathematics for emergent to advanced bilingual students. In S. Crespo, S. Celedón-Pattichis, & M. Civil (Eds.), *Access and equity: Promoting high quality mathematics in grades 3–5* (pp. 81–98). Reston, VA: National Council of Teachers of Mathematics (NCTM).

Echevarria, J., Vogt, M. E., & Short, D. (2007). *Making content comprehensible for English learners: The SIOP model* (3rd ed.). Boston, MA: Pearson Allyn & Bacon.

García, O. (2009). *Bilingual education in the 21st century: A global perspective.* Malden, MA and Oxford: Blackwell/Wiley.

Gibbons, P. (1991). *Learning to learn in a second language.* Newtown, N.S.W.: Primary English Teaching Association.

Gottlieb, M., & Ernst-Slavit, G. (2014). *Academic language in diverse classrooms: Definitions and contexts.* Thousand Oaks, CA: Corwin.

Halliday, M.A.K. (1978). *Language as social semiotic: The social interpretation of language and meaning.* London, UK: Edward Arnold.

Halliday, M. A. K. (1993). Language in a changing world. *Occasional Papers, 13,* 1–41.

Jewitt, C. (2002). The move from page to screen: The multimodal reshaping of school English. *Visual Communication, 1*(2), 171–195.

Jewitt, C., & Kress, G. (Eds.). (2003). *Multimodal literacy.* New York, NY: Peter Lang.

Kress, G., & Van Leeuwen, T. (2001). *Multimodal discourse: The modes and media of contemporary communication.* London, UK: Arnold.

The New London Group. (1996). A pedagogy of multiliteracies: Designing social futures. *Harvard Educational Review, 66*(1), 60–93.

Nodelman, P. (1988). *Words about pictures: The narrative art of children's picture books.* Athens, GA: University of Georgia Press.

Painter, C., Martin, J. R., & Unsworth, L. (2013). *Reading visual narratives: Image analysis of children's picture books*. Bristol, CT: Equinox Publishing.

Schleppegrell, M. (2004). *The language of schooling: A functional linguistics perspective*. Mahwah, NJ: Lawrence Erlbaum Associates.

Skutnabb-Kangas, T., & Toukomaa, P. (1976). *Teaching migrant children's mother tongue and learning the language of the host country in the context of the sociocultural situation of the migrant family*. Helsinki: The Finnish National Commission for UNESCO.

Valdés, G. (2010). Between support and marginalisation: The development of academic language in linguistic minority children. In J. Brutt-Griffler & M. Varghese (Eds.), *Bilingualism and language pedagogy* (pp. 10–40). Tonawanda, NY: Multilingual Matters.

Walsh, M. (2008). Worlds have collided and modes have merged: Classroom evidence of changed literacy practices. *Literacy, 42*(2), 102–108.

Walsh, M. (2009). Pedagogic potentials of multimodal literacy. In L. Tan Wee Hin, & R. Subramanian, (Eds.), *Handbook of research on new media literacy at the K–12 level: Issues and challenges* (pp. 32–47). Hershey, PA: IGI Global.

Walsh, M. (2010). Multimodal literacy: What does it mean for classroom practice? *Australian Journal of Language and Literacy, 33*(3), 211–239.

CHAPTER 4

THE POWER OF WORKING TOGETHER

Research on Collaborative Writing and Implications for Practice

Loren Jones

Collaborative writing is a strategy for writing instruction that teachers can draw on to support the writing development of their students, especially English language learners (ELLs). This chapter synthesizes and interprets the current empirical research on collaborative writing in the elementary context. At a time when educators are searching for ways to effectively support students in becoming proficient writers, this chapter puts forth a framework for teachers to implement collaborative writing in their classrooms.

Over the years, research has revealed many tools and strategies that educators can use to work effectively with ELLs. One of the strategies, often underrepresented in the research on second language writing, is the use of collaborative pairs/groups (Aminloo, 2013). Collaboration has shown to be an effective tool to support academic language development in ELLs (Wong-Fillmore & Snow, 2005), especially when students have the opportunity to interact with their fluent English-speaking

Expanding Literacy Practices Across Multiple Modes and
Languages for Multilingual Students, pages 57–71.

peers (Faltis, Arias, & Mamíez-Marín et al., 2010; Rumberger & Gándara, 2004). Collaboration can be used in conjunction with writing to help ELLs develop their writing skills, but also to help them grow individually with increased motivation and a more positive perception of themselves as legitimate writers.

Writing is of high importance as it often functions as a gateway to higher-grade levels, entry to college, and acceptance in the job market (National Commission on Writing in America's Schools and Colleges, 2003). Current assessment scores reveal that only about a quarter of students performed at or above the "proficient" level in writing on the 2011 National Assessment of Educational Progress Writing Assessment (NAEP; NCES, 2012). Most students, it appears, are performing at the 'basic level', which indicates that students demonstrate only a limited grasp of the importance of extended or complex thought (NCES, 2012). There is an obvious need for change in writing instruction, but determining which approach is most effective presents a challenge. The guide developed by Graham et al. (2012) highlights four recommendations that educators can use to make the necessary changes in order to increase writing achievement for elementary students so that they will succeed in school and society. Recommendation 4, *Create an engaged community of writers,* highlights collaborative writing as a legitimate approach for writing instruction.

Collaborative writing is defined in various ways across the literature, but a generally accepted definition is *a process in which students join efforts to develop a single text* (Graham et al., 2012). This process involves sharing, exchanging, and combining writing strategies and features of style. Collaborative writing provides students with an opportunity to improve their individual writing performance (e.g., Wong et al., 2011), learn new skills and strategies through peer interaction (e.g., Vass, 2007), gain confidence and motivation to write (e.g., Chung & Walsh, 2006), and form a more positive perception of writing (e.g., Yarrow & Topping, 2001). It's worth noting that collaborative writing, especially in the elementary context, did not garner attention until the seminal work of Dauite and Dalton was published in the late 80s and early 90s. The seminal pieces including *Do 1 and 1 make 2? Patterns of influence by collaborative authors* (1986) and *Collaboration between children learning to write: Can novices be masters?* (1992), set the groundwork for implementing collaborative writing in the classroom and paved the way for further research in this area. Following the seminal pieces, more researchers began to focus on collaborative writing in both the elementary context (e.g., Fisher, 1994; Marzano, 1990; Schultz, 1997), and in the secondary context (e.g., Dale, 1994; Keys, 1995). Since then, however, there has not been a great deal of attention given to this area of research.

This chapter highlights the main findings of a review of literature concerning collaborative writing in the elementary context, with a specific focus on ELLs. Based on the findings, the chapter then provides a framework for integrating collaborative writing in the classroom and discusses implications for teacher education and ongoing professional development. The overarching goal is to provide an overview of the theory and research behind collaborative writing and to present strategies to integrate this writing approach in the classroom.

RESEARCH ON COLLABORATIVE WRITING

Theoretical Framework

The prominent framework in research on collaborative writing in the elementary context is the sociocultural theory proposed by Vygtosky (1978). This theory was constructed in an effort to prove that social interactions enable humans to develop advanced thoughts through repeated interactions with more experienced individuals in the community (Vanderburg, 2006). Two of the most important concepts of this theory are that of internalization and the zone of proximal development (ZPD), both of which were discussed at length in many of the studies reviewed here.

The zone of proximal development (ZPD) is defined by Vygotsky as, "the distance between the actual development level as determined by the independent problem solving and the level of potential development as determined through problem solving under adult guidance or in collaboration with more capable peers" (1978, p. 86). Essentially, adults or more capable peers serve as the expert during collaborative activities as they draw on their knowledge and skills in order to engage less advanced individuals in performing at higher levels of abstraction and performance. During this process, the less advanced individual benefits a great deal from the access they have to the experts' knowledge, skills, and coaching. While many participants in the studies reviewed were paired with peers in their same class/at their same level, it should be noted that collaboration with partners who differ only slightly or differ in some domains may bring individuals part of the distance in their zone of proximal development (Daiute & Dalton, 1992).

The process of internalization occurs during collaboration when, through verbal interaction, the individual develops an inner voice that monitors the learning of new tasks and concepts. This concept involves making individual the knowledge and processes that occur during collaboration in such a way that it becomes an internal mental function (Vygotsky, 1978, p. 89). Oftentimes during collaboration, students think out loud which provides an opportunity for self-reflection as well as an opportunity for peer feedback. It is during this time of discussion and reflection that individuals have the opportunity to further develop his/her inner voice. It is important to note that the concepts of ZPD and internalization are intertwined with one another as individuals often go through this process of internalization when they are interacting with experts in their ZPD.

Method of Literature Review

The review of literature was guided by one central question: *What are the benefits of implementing collaborative writing as an instructional strategy in an elementary classroom with ELLs?*

Based on the central question, studies for review were selected that met the following criteria: (1) studied collaborative writing, including brief interventions as well as longer studies, (2) included evaluation of writing outcome and/or evaluation of writing processes, (3) published in a peer-reviewed journal or book in English (year 2000-present), (4) included participants at the Elementary (primary) level (K–6). It should be noted that studies with first-language and second-language writing were included. In addition, I included studies that were conducted in a traditional classroom setting (paper and pencil) and studies that were conducted in a more modern setting (technology). Studies were excluded that took place in a setting outside of the school classroom. In total, 18 studies were found to meet the inclusion criteria.

The focus of this review was to develop an understanding of how collaborative writing has been used in elementary classrooms, in some cases with ELLs, in order to develop a framework for other teachers to use this writing approach in their classrooms. With this focus in mind, I analyzed each study to note research foci, theoretical perspectives, context (location of the study), participant characteristics (class size, age of students, primary language, etc.), study design, type of collaboration (pairs/groups, type of written product), and results of the collaboration. A review of the results of the collaboration from each study revealed commonalities across the studies which I used to develop the framework.

In the following sections of this chapter, I highlight the commonalities identified across the 18 studies on collaborative writing in the elementary context. The commonalities appear in order of prevalence and include detailed examples from the various studies. The chapter then presents a proposed framework for classroom teachers and will come to a close with implications for literacy teacher education.

LITERATURE REVIEW FINDINGS

Learning Writing Skills Through Peer Interaction

The first commonality, identified in almost all of the reviewed studies, is students learning writing skills through peer interaction. Researchers revealed that through peer interaction, students helped one another to learn new writing skills and strategies, which influenced them to make modifications to their own writing, resulting in improvements (e.g., Li, Chu, & Ki, 2014; Topping et al., 2000; Woo et al., 2011). The "helping" component occurred through various processes across the studies. Many studies showed that students helped one another through joint planning in which they shared, explored, and integrated ideas (Rojas-Drummond, Albarrán, & Littleton, 2008; Vass, 2007; Yarrow & Topping, 2001). Other studies revealed that students helped one another by providing comments and corrective feedback (Li et al., 2012; Woo et al., 2011; Woo, Chu, & Li, 2013; Yate et al., 2013,). The improvements observed as a direct result of peer interaction ranged from adding new ideas (Woo et al., 2011) to writing more appropriate words and sentences (Li et al., 2014).

A seminal study from Daiute (1986) revealed that through collaboration, children teach each other ways of thinking about the writing process and specifics about text form. In this specific case, Brian and John (working together on a collaborative writing task) each brought their own unique skills/writing preferences to the task assigned, which resulted in them "rubbing off" on one another. For example, Brian used extensive dialogue in his posttest when he used none in his pretest. This was a clear influence from his partner, John, in the writing process. In a different, more current study, Roberts and Eady (2012) showed that through conferencing sessions, students were able to draw on several suggestions made by their peers in order to improve their writing skills. During these sessions, students shared ideas, made suggestions for content revisions, suggestions for spelling/grammar improvements, etc. As a result of these collaborative sessions, students were able to apply their newly acquired skills to their individual writing.

The majority of the studies on collaborative writing in the elementary context showed that students benefit from the collaborative writing process by learning writing skills through peer interaction. These writing skills vary across the studies, however, many of the studies showed that students were able to think critically with one another in order to generate new ideas, expand their vocabulary, and focus on details such as punctuation and spelling.

Improved Writing Performance

Across the studies, a majority of researchers cited improved writing performance as a result of the collaborative writing. The improvement was determined using different criteria depending on the goals of the study. In some instances, improvements were determined by linguistic complexity, rhetorical structure, features of style, and holistic quality (Daiute,1986) whereas other studies looked at vocabulary and story elements (Roberts & Eady, 2012). Most of the studies that cited improved writing performance highlighted increases in writing scores that showed statistical significance (Li et al., 2012; Nixon & Topping, 2001; Topping et al., 2000; Woo, Chu, & Li, 2013; Yarrow & Topping, 2001).

The widely-cited study from Daiute and Dalton (1992) examined writing performance in terms of story elements. These story elements included setting, character attributes and feelings, climax, problems, dialogue, explanations, etc. The researchers compared the use of story elements in students' pre- and post-collaboration stories and found that 11 of 14 children increased their use of story elements. Results from this study demonstrated that indirect instruction from peers, as opposed to explicit modeling from the teacher, is especially powerful.

A more recent study from Wong et al. (2011) focused on collaborative writing through group Wiki pages. Prior to the collaborative writing, teachers identified problems in the students' writing, including limited and incorrect use of vocabulary, English-style grammar, badly structured passages, and so on. After the collaborative writing, the year 4, L2 students in this study achieved significant improvement in every assessed skill for writing including punctuation marks, characters, sentences, organization, structure, content and words. Students indicated that they were more motivated to help each other when they worked in groups, as they felt less threatened when they made mistakes.

The improved writing performance was shown by the majority of studies through the statistically significant increase in writing scores from pre- to post-collaborative writing. The study from Roberts and Eady (2012) did not include statistical information, but instead explained how students' writing improved with more ambitious words, sentences with more interesting openings, an increase in adjectives, adverbs, similes, and personification to enhance description.

Many of the studies in this review highlighted the improved writing performance of students participating in the collaborative writing activities. While some studies captured this improvement by comparing writing scores across time, others took a more specified approach, and examined particular writing elements for signs of improvement. Overall, no matter the approach to analysis, the collaborative writing activities were shown to improve students' writing performance.

Increased Motivation and Self-Efficacy

Many of the reviewed studies reported increased motivation and self-efficacy as a result of the collaborative writing activities. Various factors contributed to the observed increase in motivation and self-efficacy, however the two main elements were the opportunity to incorporate personal experiences and the opportunity to work in partners/groups. By encouraging students to incorporate their personal experiences in their writing, students were able to take ownership of their writing and feel encouraged (Yate et al., 2013). Working in partners/groups allowed students to improve in their weaker skills while also helping others in their stronger areas which led to students' increase in confidence and self-esteem (Topping et al., 2000; Wong et al., 2011; Yarrow & Topping, 2001).

The study from Chung and Walsh (2006) focused on the peer collaboration of kindergarten and first grade students during a computer-writing project that spanned two school semesters. During the project, students collaboratively produced a total of four stories. Over the course of the project, researchers observed the interaction patterns of children changing from a more independent style to a more integrative style. In addition, researchers observed a shift in role patterns so that children began alternating the roles of leader and observer with less competent children beginning to carry out more important tasks. Throughout the project, the writing tasks encouraged students to work together, which resulted in increased motivation and willingness to work in this particular study.

A number of the studies revealed that by participating in the collaborative writing activities, students' motivation and self-efficacy increased. Though the context of these studies differed, researchers revealed that students felt more confident in their writing abilities after collaborating with their peers on the assigned writing tasks. In some cases, students even began to assert themselves as writers by taking on more of a lead role in the interaction, which is a testament to their increased motivation and self-efficacy.

Positive Perception of Writing

Researchers from several of the studies indicated that students developed a more positive perception of writing. This perception was observed and, in some cases, measured via survey (Hertz-Lazarowitz & Bar-Natan, 2002; Li et al., 2014; Roberts & Eady, 2012; Wong et al., 2011). Many of the researchers indicated that the positive perception of writing was observed through students showing excitement and enthusiasm for continuing to write collaboratively (Topping et al., 2000; Yarrow & Topping, 2001). In addition, many studies cited better attitudes as an indicator of the positive perception of writing (Li et al., 2012).

The study from Nixon and Topping (2001) examined the impact of paired writing between emergent writers and older children with a writing delay. Researchers found that the change regarding attitudes measured pre- to post-intervention was highly statistically significant. In addition, teachers noted a visible difference in the whole class ethos due to this positive change in attitude.

Hertz-Lazarowitz & Bar-Natan (2002) showcased an increase in students' perception of writing as one of their most significant findings. The authors revealed that the students made remarkable gains in the survey used to test their perception of writing with computers. What made this finding even more significant is that the survey indicated that the collaborative writing environment equalized and significantly enriched the experience for Arabs and girls, students who typically experience less gain.

Though captured in different ways, many of the studies found that students' perception of writing was more positive after engaging in the collaborative writing activities. This is an important finding, as it can impact the way students approach writing activities in the future, both in collaborative and independent settings.

Technology as a Supportive Tool in the Collaborative Process

A number of the studies implemented collaborative writing within a technology-based platform such as Microsoft applications (power point, word), online wikis and shareware (e.g., 'goldwave'). The affordances of the technology varied from study to study, but the majority indicated that technology served as a tool for support and enrichment of students' writing products and writing processes.

Rojas-Drummond et al. (2008) presented an interesting case in which fourth grade students from Mexico worked in groups to write a text. The groups planned, discussed and wrote several drafts of their story which they later re-constructed and polished to create a complete written version via word processor. The students enriched their stories using pictures, animation, voice, and music with the help of Power Point, the Internet and shareware such as 'goldwave.' In this case, the technology served as a tool of enrichment that allowed students to turn their written text into a multimedia product.

The study from Li et al. (2012) is different in that the technology is used as a tool to support the writing processes of participating students. The study took place at a primary school in China in which students worked in collaborative groups of four to produce a written text. The students used a wiki-based writing environment called Joyous Writing club (JWC) to complete their assigned writing task. Researchers found that the program increased group interactions and extended the audience for the students' writing. The technology provided a way for students to communicate more as they could write at any time (during and after class) and it was easier for peer edits, revision and comments. Though the platforms differed, studies that employed technology for collaborative writing found that the technology served as a supportive tool for students to engage in the writing activities.

DISCUSSION

The goal of this review was to present the commonalities found across studies on collaborative writing in the elementary context in order to show what has been done thus far and to construct a framework for teachers based on this information. Across the eighteen studies reviewed here, five commonalities emerged, each contributing to the construction of the framework and implications for literacy teacher education.

Research revealed that students benefit greatly from participating in collaborative writing activities. Some of these benefits were directly related to writing ability (e.g., improved writing performance) while others related to development and growth of the individual (e.g., increased self-efficacy). Through the process of collaborative writing, students shared and integrated ideas, argued their points of view, negotiated and coordinated perspectives, asked for and provided opinions, etc. Research showed that through these actions students often learned new writing strategies and skills, which led to improvement in their writing performance. In addition, students often experienced an increase in motivation and self-efficacy, which contributed to a more positive perception of writing. Many of the studies also showcased the affordances of technology as a tool for support and enrichment of students' writing products and writing processes.

The benefits of collaborative writing, as identified above, provide support for collaborative writing as an instructional practice in the elementary context. It is evident, based on my search for studies that this instructional practice has not yet "picked up steam", but the evidence presented here shows its potential to help students both academically (learn new writing skills, improved writing performance) and socially (increase in motivation and self-efficacy).

EXPANDING LITERACY PRACTICES: CLASSROOM STRATEGIES

The findings from this review of literature help to establish collaborative writing as a legitimate strategy for teaching writing at the elementary level. Across the studies, collaborative writing was implemented differently, from using a paired writing model to using a wiki-based writing environment. Although very different approaches, these two forms of implementation (along with numerous others presented in the studies) have similarities that can be used to form a framework for collaborative writing to be used across grade levels and content areas. The framework, shown in Figure 3.1, is a step-by-step guide that teachers can use to implement this writing approach in their classrooms. It should be noted that the writing process is cyclical, nonlinear, and iterative in nature (Li et al., 2012; Rojas Drummond, 2008; Yarrow & Topping, 2001). Although the framework is presented in numbered steps (below), I encourage teachers to go back and forth between the steps, as needed, in order to meet the needs of their students.

1. Introduce the Collaborative Writing Process: The classroom teacher should begin by explaining what collaborative writing is and the purpose

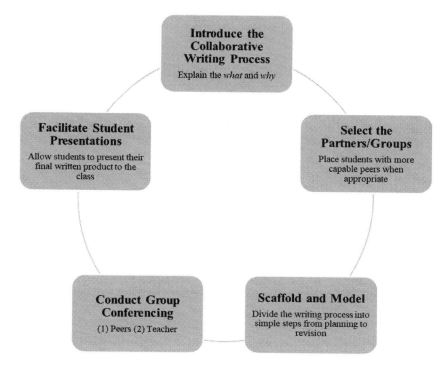

FIGURE 3.1. Framework for a collaborative writing approach to writing instruction.

it serves so that students have an understanding of what they will be doing with their partner(s) and why. (This is a step that teachers may need to revisit as students become acclimated to writing in this way.)

2. Select the Partners/Groups: The teacher should be purposeful in selecting the partners/groups for collaborative writing as previous studies have highlighted uncooperative pairs/groups as a major challenge (e.g., Roberts & Eady, 2012; Yarrow & Topping, 2001). This step will require careful consideration from teachers as some studies have shown that pairing students with a more capable peer results in significant improvements for both students (e.g., Topping et al., 2000) while others have shown that mixed ability groups is the most effective participant structure for collaborative writing activities (e.g., Rojas-Drummond et al., 2008).

3. Scaffold and Model: After selecting partners/groups, the teacher needs to scaffold the writing process for students, especially when doing collaborative writing for the first time. Through scaffolding the teacher can divide the collaborative writing process into simple steps that students will be able to follow. The teacher should model the different writing steps for the students, focusing on the collaborative aspects in order to prevent students from maintaining their individual working habits. Teachers can model in the form of a "think aloud" where the teacher walks students through exactly what they can expect at the different stages of writing from planning to revision.

4. Conduct Group Conferencing: After the writing is completed, the teacher should implement 'group conferencing' as a form of collaboration between the pairs/groups of students and their peers and the pairs/groups of students and the teacher. The first part of group conferencing allows the pairs/groups of students to present their writing and get feedback from other peers regarding content, format, etc. The second part of group conferencing allows students to work with the teacher, so they can provide support in the revision process before they create their final product.

5. Facilitate Student Presentations: The final step is for the teacher to encourage students to present their final product to the class and other relevant community members (administrators, other teachers, parents, etc.).

With all assignments and activities, especially in the current era of testing, the assessment portion can present a challenge. For the collaborative writing activity, this is most definitely the case as teachers are presented with a final product that is a blend of different contributions from each writer (Diaute, 1986). There are methods, however, that can be used to ensure that all students receive a grade representative of their contributions along with feedback to help further their individual development. For example, in one of the studies reviewed here (Ferguson-Patrick, 2007) the teacher instructed students to each use a different colored pencil when writing for purposes of individual accountability. This allowed the teacher to accurately grade the students and to give each one of them feedback according to their strengths/weaknesses shown in the written text. A different method of assessment is to have students fill out a questionnaire in which they answer questions based on their specific contributions to the writing task. The teacher, after reviewing the questionnaire responses, can meet with each student to review their grade, strengths/weaknesses, and provide recommendations for their future writing.

IMPLICATIONS FOR LITERACY TEACHER EDUCATION

Previous research has shown that *all* teachers, not just ESOL specialists or bilingual professionals, need to be prepared to work with ELLs (Lucas & Grinberg, 2008). This is especially important now as teachers are seeing a rapid increase in the ELL population in classrooms across the United States (U.S. Department of Education, National Center for Education Statistics [NCES], 2016). Teacher educators, currently under a great deal of pressure to adequately prepare teachers to work with ELLs (Athanases & de Oliviera, 2011), can utilize the framework proposed here in their classrooms as one approach to writing instruction. This framework, although designed with a focus on ELLs, can be highly effective for all students as previous research on collaborative writing has shown (e.g., Roberts & Eady, 2012).

Incorporating this framework in teacher education programs can be accomplished in the context of a course on literacy instruction or even in a methods course designed for teaching English as a second language (ESOL). I recommend introducing this framework for collaborative writing using the the genre-based approach to writing instruction focused on the Teaching-Learning cycle (TLC) (de Oliviera & Lan, 2014; Martin & Rose, 2008). The TLC (Brisk, 2015; de Oliviera, 2017) is made up of four phases of activity: deconstruction, joint construction, collaborative construction, and independent construction. Each of these phases is based on the premise that the knowledge developed about language through reading can be used within writing instruction through modeling and guidance in the context of a shared experience.

During the first phase of activity, joint construction, teachers introduce a mentor text in a chosen genre that students are expected to read and write. Teachers guide students in the deconstruction of the mentor text through modeling and discussions regarding the purpose and structure of the text, and language features commonly found in the genre. This deconstruction process supports students as they build on their knowledge of language and content.

The second phase of activity, joint construction, is a time in which teachers work with students to co-construct a text of the same genre as the deconstructed mentor text. The teacher guides the writing process (scribing while stuents write on their own paper), encouraging students to contribute ideas for content, sentence structure, language choice, and more. There is a specific focus on using the structure and language features that were introduced and discussed during the deconstruction phase. This is a crucial phase of activity as teachers provide scaffolding between students' every day, conversational language and the academic language of school.

The third phrase of activity, collaborative construction, is the basis of this chapter. During this time the teacher should utilize the framework put forth here (Figure 4.1) to navigate students through the writing process as they work with a peer to co-construct a single text. The teacher must be explicit when giving instructions and modeling the collaborative writing process (step 1). This is often achieved through a think-aloud in which the teacher demonstrates how partners work effectively to produce a single written text. Students should be placed with partners according to their academic level and social characteristics (step 2). Research has shown that placing students of mixed abilities together can benefit each student. The social characteristics come into play as the teacher decides which personalities will be productive together. After partners have been selected and the collaborative writing process has been explained, it is beneficial for teachers to break down the writing task into simple steps. This can be achieved through planning sheets, graphic organizers, sentence starters, and more (step 3). It is also important for teachers to refer students back to the deconstructed mentor text and jointly constructed text for guidance as the collaboratively written text will be in the same genre. After students have worked together to produce a single text, conferencing will take place (step 4). During this time the peers will work with other classmates to revise their work by soliciting feedback based on content, spelling, sentence structure, etc. After students work with one another, the teacher will meet individually with each set of partners to revise their work one final time. As the final step in collaborative construction, students will present their writing to the class, school, and/or community (step 5).

The fourth and final phase of the TLC is independent construction. During this phase, students work individually to construct their own texts in the specified genre. Teachers are expected to keep their scaffolding and guidance to a minimum so that students have the opportunity to write independently using the knowledge and skills they developed throughout the first three phrases of the Teaching-Learning cycle.

The TLC provides a rich context for introducing collaborative writing to preservice teachers. Although collaborative writing can be used on its own as an approach to writing instruction, it's beneficial to present it in this way so that students have adequate support and scaffolding in the specified genre.

The findings from the review of research highlight collaborative writing as a legitimate writing instruction strategy that can help students find success, both in their development as writers and as individuals. The framework presented, especially when used in the context of the Teaching-Learning Cycle (TLC), offers teachers and teacher educators an accessible way to facilitate collaborative writing across content areas and grade levels.

REFLECTION QUESTIONS

1. How might collaborative writing be implemented in your classroom?
2. What other affordances does the TLC provide teachers and students, beyond what was described in this chapter?
3. How do the ideas presented in this chapter apply to your specific teaching context?

REFERENCES

Aminloo, M. S. (2013). The effective of collaborative writing on EFL learners writing ability at the elementary level. *Journal of Language Teaching & Research, 4*(4), 801–806.

Athanases, S. Z., & de Oliviera, L. C. (2011). Toward program-wide coherence in preparing teachers to teach and advocate for English language learners. In T. Lucas (Ed.), *Teacher preparation for linguistically diverse classrooms: A resource for teacher educators* (pp. 195–215). New York, NY: Routledge.

Brisk, M. E. (2015). *Engaging students in academic literacies: Genre-based pedagogy for K–5 classrooms.* New York, NY: Routledge.

Chung, Y. H., & Walsh, D. J. (2006). Constructing a joint story-writing space: The dynamics of young children's collaboration at computers. Early Education and Development, 17(3), 373–420. Retrieved from http://dx.doi.org/10.1207/s15566935eed1703_4

Daiute, C. (1986). Do 1 and 1 make 2? Patterns of influence by collaborative authors. *Written Communication, 3*(3), 382–408. https://doi.org/10.1177/0741088386003003006

Daiute, C., & Dalton, B. (1992). Collaboration between children learning to write: Can novices be masters? *Cognition and Instruction, 10,* 281–333. Retrieved from http://dx.doi.org/10.1207/s1532690xci1004_1

Dale, H. (1994). Collaborative writing interactions in one ninth-grade classroom. *The Journal of Educational Research, 87*(6), 334–344. Retrieved from http://dx.doi.org/10.1080/00220671.1994.9941264

de Oliveira, L. C. (2017). *A genre-based approach to L2 writing instruction in K–12. TESOL Connections.* Retrieved from http://newsmanager.commpartners.com/tesolc/downloads/features/2017/2017-07-TLC.pdf

de Oliveira, L. C., & Lan, S. (2014). Writing science in an upper elementary classroom: A genre-based approach to teaching English language learners. *Journal of Second Language Writing, 25,* 23–39. Retrieved from https://doi.org/10.1016/j.jslw.2014.05.001

Faltis, C., Arias, M. B., & Ramírez-Marín, F. (2010). Identifying relevant competencies for secondary teachers of English learners. *Bilingual Research Journal, 33*(3), 307–328. Retrieved from http://dx.doi.org/10.1080/15235882.2010.529350

Ferguson-Patrick, K. (2007). Writers develop skills through collaboration: an action research approach. *Educational Action Research, 15*(2), 159–180. Retrieved from https://doi.org/10.1080/09650790701314585

Fisher, E. (1994). Joint composition at the computer: Learning to talk about writing. *Computers and Composition, 11*(3), 251–262. Retrieved from https://doi.org/10.1016/8755-4615(94)90017-5

Graham, S., Bolinger, A., Olson, C. B., D'Aoust, C., MacArthur, C. A., McCutchen, D., & Olinghouse, N. (2012). *Teaching elementary school students to be effective writers: A practice guide.* (NCEE 2012–4058). Washington, DC: National Center for Education Evaluation and Regional Assistance, Institute of Education Sciences, U.S. Department of Education. Retrieved from http://ies.ed.gov/ncee/wwc/publications_reviews.aspx#pubsearch

Hertz-Lazarowitz, R., & Bar-Natan, I. (2002). Writing development of Arab and Jewish students using cooperative learning (CL) and computer-mediated communication (CMC). *Computers & Education, 39*(1), 19–36. Retrieved from https://doi.org/10.1016/S0360-1315(02)00019-2

Keys, C. W. (1995). An interpretive study of students' use of scientific reasoning during a collaborative report writing intervention in ninth grade general science. *Science Education, 79*(4), 415–435. Retrieved from doi:10.1002/sce.3730790405

Li, X., Chu, S. K. W., & Ki, W. W. (2014). The effects of a wiki-based collaborative process writing pedagogy on writing ability and attitudes among upper primary school students in mainland China. *Computers & Education, 77*, 151–169. Retrieved from https://doi.org/10.1016/j.compedu.2014.04.019

Li, X., Chu, S. K. W., Ki, W. W., & Woo, M. (2012). Using a wiki-based collaborative process writing pedagogy to facilitate collaborative writing among Chinese primary school students. Australasian Journal of Educational Technology, 28(1), 159–181. Retrieved from http://hdl.handle.net/10722/159995

Lucas, T., & Grinberg, J. (2008) Responding to the linguistic reality of mainstream classrooms: Preparing all teachers to teach English language learners. In M. Cochran-Smith, S. Feiman-Nemser, D. J. McIntyre, & K. E. Demers (Eds.), *Handbook of research on teacher education: Enduring questions in changing contexts* (3rd ed., pp. 606–636). New York, NY: Routledge.

Martin, J. R., & Rose, D. (2008). *Genre relations: Mapping culture.* London, UK: Equinox.

Marzano, L. (1990). Connecting literature with cooperative writing (in the classroom). *Reading Teacher, 43*(6), 429–430.

National Center for Education Statistics (2012). *The Nation's Report Card: Writing 2011* (NCES 2012–470). Institute of Education Sciences, U.S. Department of Education, Washington, D.C. Retrieved from https://nces.ed.gov/nationsreportcard/pdf/main2011/2012470.pdf

National Commission on Writing in America's Schools and Colleges. (2003). *The neglected R: The need for a writing revolution.* New York, NY: College Entrance Examination Board.

Nixon, J. G., & Topping, K. J. (2001). Emergent writing: The impact of structured peer interaction. *Educational Psychology, 21*(1), 41–58. Retrieved from https://doi.org/10.1080/01443410123268

Roberts, J., & Eady, S. (2012). Enhancing the quality of learning: what are the benefits of a mixed age, collaborative approach to creative narrative writing? *Education 3–13, 40*(2), 205–216. Retrieved from http://dx.doi.org/10.1080/03004279.2010.511624

Rojas-Drummond, S. M., Albarrán, C. D., & Littleton, K. S. (2008). Collaboration, creativity and the co-construction of oral and written texts. *Thinking skills and creativity, 3*(3), 177–191. Retrieved from https://doi.org/10.1016/j.tsc.2008.09.008

Rumberger, R. W., & Gándara, P. (2004). Seeking equity in the education of California's English learners. *Teachers College Record, 106*(10), 2032–2056.

Schultz, K. (1997). "Do you want to be in my story?": Collaborative writing in an urban elementary classroom. *Journal of Literacy Research, 29*(2), 253–287. Retrieved from https://doi.org/10.1080/10862969709547958

Topping, K., Nixon, J., Sutherland, J., & Yarrow, F. (2000). Paired writing: A framework for effective collaboration. *Reading, 34*(2), 79–89. doi:10.1111/1467-9345.00139

U.S. Department of Education, National Center for Education Statistics (2016). *Number and percentage of public school students participating in English language learner (ELL) programs, by state: Selected years, fall 2004 through fall 2014.* Washington, DC: Government Printing Office. Retrieved from https://nces.ed.gov/programs/digest/d16/tables/dt16_204.20.asp

Vanderburg, R. M. (2006). Reviewing research on teaching writing based on Vygotsky's theories: What we can learn. *Reading & Writing Quarterly, 22*(4), 375–393. Retrieved from https://doi.org/10.1080/10573560500455778

Vass, E. (2007). Exploring processes of collaborative creativity—The role of emotions in children's joint creative writing. *Thinking Skills and Creativity, 2*(2), 107–117. Retrieved from https://doi.org/10.1016/j.tsc.2007.06.001

Vygotsky, L.S. (1978). *Mind in society: The development of higher psychological processes.* Cambridge, MA: Harvard University Press.

Woo, M. M., Chu, S. K. W., Ho, A., & Li, X. (2011). Using a wiki to scaffold primary-school students' collaborative writing. *Educational Technology & Society, 14*(1), 43–54. Retrieved from http://www.jstor.org/stable/jeductechsoci.14.1.43

Woo, M. M., Chu, S. K. W., & Li, X. (2013). Peer-feedback and revision process in a wiki mediated collaborative writing. *Educational Technology Research and Development, 61*(2), 279–309. Retrieved from https://doi.org/10.1007/s11423-012-9285-y

Wong, L. H., Chen, W., Chai, C. S., Chin, C. K., & Gao, P. (2011). A blended collaborative writing approach for Chinese L2 primary school students. *Australasian Journal of Educational Technology, 27*(7), 1208–1226. Retrieved from https://doi.org/10.14742/ajet.913

Wong-Fillmore, L., & Snow, C. (2005). What teachers need to know about language. In C. T. Adger, C. E. Snow, & D. Christian (Eds.), *What teachers need to know about language* (pp. 7–54). Washington, DC: Center for Applied Linguistics.

Yarrow, F., & Topping, K. J. (2001). Collaborative writing: The effects of metacognitive prompting and structured peer interaction. *British Journal of Educational Psychology, 71*(2), 261–282. doi:10.1348/000709901158514

Yate González, Y. Y., Saenz, L. F., Bermeo, J. A., & Castañeda Chaves, A. F. (2013). The role of collaborative work in the development of elementary students' writing skills. *PROFILE: Issues in Teachers' Professional Development, 15*(1), 11–25. Retrieved from http://www.scielo.org.co/scielo.php?script=sci_arttext&pid=S1657-

CHAPTER 5

TRANSLANGUAGING WRITING PRACTICES AND IMPLICATIONS FOR MULTILINGUAL STUDENTS

Carolina Rossato de Almeida

Given that bilingual students are the fastest growing population in United States' schools, understanding the influence of language in their literacy development is crucial in order to improve teaching and learning methods for a diverse classroom. The goal of this chapter is to review the literature on translanguaging as a writing practice and offer insights on its benefits, suggestions on how to incorporate creative assignments in the classroom, and implications and considerations for teachers. This chapter concludes with some questions that remain regarding the implementation of translanguaging as pedagogy.

The ability of moving across languages and across registers of speech is known as *translanguaging*, or the "bilingual practice of accessing different linguistic features or various modes of what are described as autonomous languages in order to maximize communicative potential" (Garcia, 2009, p. 140). The term captures the essence of language as a verb rather than a noun and something people do rather than possess (Sayer, 2013). The prefix "trans," which means to transcend, differentiates the term *translanguaging* from *code-switching* and *code-mixing*, and sug-

Expanding Literacy Practices Across Multiple Modes and Languages for Multilingual Students, pages 73–81.

gests that speakers go beyond language boundaries in order to express themselves (Otheguy, 2016). Students who speak multiple languages use their multilingual knowledge to make sense of their worlds and in their writing (Garcia & Sylvan, 2011; Sayer, 2013).

Composing between languages was traditionally frowned upon in educational settings (Creese & Blackledge, 2010). However, new research on translanguaging demonstrates that knowledge of one or more languages coalesces and may have a positive effect in students' writing (Kabuto, 2010; Pacheco & Goodwin, 2013). Given that bilingual/multilingual students are the fastest growing population in United States' classrooms, understanding their literacy development is crucial in order to improve teaching and learning methods for a diverse group (Blake, 2001; Ebe & Chapman-Santiago, 2016). This review offers insight on the use of translanguaging, including how to expand literacy practices in the classroom as well as implications for teachers.

This chapter encompasses a sociocultural approach to the use of language, and regards it as a tool for thinking and making sense of the world (Vygotsky, 1962). People's literacy practices are situated in broad social relations and historical contexts (Razfar & Gutiérrez, 2003). Multilingual perspectives and practices include validation of students' cultural and linguistic backgrounds as resources for learning, and an understanding of the role of primary language in the acquisition of a new language (Gort, 2006). Thus, affording students with opportunities to draw from their home language to write and compose texts should be seen as a resource as opposed to a limitation.

RESEARCH ON TRANSLANGUAGING

The practice of translanguaging embodies the notion of windows and mirrors theorized by Gutiérrez (2007). Students learn about others' languages and cultures and thus become respectful and aware individuals with knowledge of the worlds outside their own (windows). This, combined with identity formation and consistent personal connection to the learning materials (mirror) becomes key in making learning accessible, relevant, and pleasant. Knowledge of more than one language can benefit any student population (Scott, 2008). Ideally, all students should be fluent in a language other than their native one given its many benefits, such as understanding and empathizing with a wide diversity of people (Nieto, 2009).

Translanguaging appears to have positive effects on a child's ability to learn (Woodley & Brown, 2016). The practice allows students to utilize knowledge from their social worlds and express themselves through different language modes in order to increase their ability to convey meaning. Bilingual students utilize inputs from both languages in their writing and possess other linguistic advantages over their monolingual peers. For instance, they pay closer attention to phoneme, phoneme length, and which sounds pertain to which written language when compared to a monolingual child (Kokkola, 2013).

Translanguaging also affords students with many social benefits, such as sharing and being proud of their identity. Encouraging students to share their backgrounds can stimulate a positive learning environment not only for bilingual/multilingual students, but also for all students who are learning that people's cultures and languages should be valued and respected (Williams, 2002). In the school environment, students often experience moments of success and failure. This is a social process that guides their behavior, thinking, and ultimately their perceptions of themselves and self-esteem (Garcia & Wei, 2014). Since translanguaging enables meaningful participation, bilingual students can use their multiple languages to invest in academic learning, thus resulting in more "success" stories and less "failures" (Palmer, 2008). Translanguaging writing assignments can be motivating for students, since it allows them to share part of their identity with others (Sfard & Prusak, 2005). Being able to use different language capitals for expression purposes allows bilingual/multilingual students to share more enhanced meaning in their writing and part of their identity.

Another way that translanguaging as a practice may promote social development is by reinforcing students' literacy in their home language. When writing in their second language, bilingual students cannot automatically divorce the voice of their first language from the writing process in their second language (Garcia & Wei, 2014). Many students know how to communicate verbally in their native language, but not how to formally read and write it, since English is the main language taught and emphasized in schools. Students should be encouraged to explore with phonetics and translanguaging in their writing, which has been associated as a positive practice that foster students' native language while developing their English skills. For example, during a Spanish writing assignment highlighted in Nichols and Colon's study (2000), a student completed her writing assignment using words in Spanish with her knowledge of English phonetics. The student used what she knew in both languages for the development and understanding of formal Spanish, which she knew how to speak fluently, but never how to write.

The practice of translanguaging is also known as receptive and nonjudgmental of language use. For example, when it comes to learning a second language, translation has been regarded as problematic and therefore discouraged. However, the notion of translanguaging welcomes the practice of translation with open arms (Celic & Seltzer, 2011). For instance, if bilingual writers, during beginning stages of writing development, are forced to think solely in English without having a grasp of the basics of the language, this could constrain their thinking capacity, limit expression, and generate frustration. If teachers make bilinguals wait to engage in meaningful writing until they develop English (or another language) proficiently, the lack of practice in engaging with deeper thoughts may result in decline of their newly gained skills as writers (Fu, 2009). Since the assumption behind translanguaging is for one to utilize all his language resources, translating should be positively reinforced in certain assignments, instead of shunned upon.

Translanguaging is an adaptive practice that can be used in a variety of contexts through different modes and tools. New technological advancements have brought digital outlets in multimodal writing to the forefront. A mode is a social and cultural resource utilized for meaning making, such as drawing images, writing, speaking, moving, acting, as well as other artifacts (Bezemer & Kress, 2008, p. 6). New technologies have enabled the production of more fluid language texts that break free from the traditional paper and pencil mode (Sebba, 2012). Many of today's children and adolescents rely heavily on multimodality as a means of communication—including image, sound, movement, text, and gesture. That is a powerful way in which people are able to connect with others and display their identities (Smith, 2014). The layering of modes may be an innovative way of allowing students to express their identities in ways not typically afforded by written texts (Smith, Pacheco, & Almeida, 2017). Combining multimodality with translanguaging can encourage students to draw from their cultural and linguistic heritages as a source of knowledge through their composition of multiple modes, using their creativity while learning a new language and maintaining their own (Ghiso & Low, 2012).

Examples such as these have important implications for teachers, especially literacy educators. When teachers scaffold literacy learning in a way that instills curiosity and is engaging for their students, writing can be seen as a liberating force. Even though many teachers find it appealing to use translanguaging practices in their classroom, they often feel constrained by the prevailing unquestioned acceptance of a monolingual ideology. English-only instruction restricts the range of pedagogical methods available to teachers, thus it is unlikely that schools will accommodate translanguaging as a legitimate practice (Garcia & Wei, 2013). Despite those limitations, teachers must take a more active stance to implement translanguaging activities in their classrooms. The following segment will discuss classroom strategies that educators can implement in the classroom and help teachers leverage the writing experience of their students.

EXPANDING LITERACY PRACTICES: CLASSROOM STRATEGIES

There are a few strategies classroom teachers can use in order to put translanguaging into practice while following the common core standards. First, teachers can allow their students to draft an assignment in their home language and then translate it to English. A bilingual/multilingual student might freeze at the daunting task of having to write solely in English because it constrains their thinking capacity and limits their expression. However, if students are told that they can draft in their home language, they tend to begin writing immediately, and do not feel constrained. Students who compose in their second language may feel less cognitive demand, and even become proud of their literary piece, as this example highlights (Fu, 2009):

Pasado semana, yo took digital storytelling. Nosotras sat en cojin sillas en lugar con aire acondicionado. Ahora, yo dar ESL escritura. Nosotras tenuos duro sillas. Le luger ne tenuous pas aire acondicionado. Le tempa es La liente et Humedo. UNH necessidad puia comprar nuero suavo sillas atencion carecer de aire acondicionado as much. (*English translation: Last week, I took digital storytelling. We sat in cushioned seats in a room with air conditionioning. Now, I take ESL writing. We have hard seats. The room is not air-conditioned. The weather is hot and humid. UNH needs to buy new soft chairs. If we had soft chairs, we would not notice the lack of air-conditioning as much*) (p. 28).

Teaching writing is essentially teaching students how to think, or to select appropriate topics, focus, organize ideas, and elaborate on important details (Fu, 2009). Hence, allowing students to translate from their drafts enables them to think through and organize a text.

Teachers can also conduct a teacher-mediated translanguaging writing assignment that is planned and structured. They may incorporate a language experience approach in their classroom that fits with the CCSS standards: First, students must have some kind of shared experience (possibly a text they have all read) from which they will develop a narrative. Then, as a whole class, the teacher may elicit the students' account of this experience and ask them to give their opinions and share their thoughts in whatever language they feel most comfortable with. The students dictate the experience to the teacher, who scribes word for word, making no corrections or edits and acting solely as a scribe. If the teacher does not know how to write in a particular language, students may be encouraged to write on the board themselves. Third, the teacher reads back the text that is written on the board to the students, who can make changes/additions to the written product. Finally, the teacher uses the final product as a text through which language and content can be taught (for example, if the experience lacks descriptive language, the teacher might ask students add descriptive language). The translanguaging component might emerge during the dictating/scribing stage as students are allowed the freedom to use both of their languages to recount their experiences (Celic & Seltzer, 2011).

Translanguaging through multimodal activities can be used as an instructional strategy to bolster comprehension of complex materials (Collins & Cioe-Pena, 2016). For instance, students may use translanguaging in their texts for specific literary effects (García & Wei, 2013). Many bilingual authors include words, phrases, and sentences in another language in their writing as a way to express their voice, to add authenticity, to express an idea that is better communicated in a particular language, or for other specific purposes (Celic & Seltzer, 2011). Practicing translanguaging for literary effect can be done in the classroom. The teacher can mediate a discussion in her classroom by showing students mentor texts where the author combines English and another language, as the following example highlights:

> With two ways of saying everything I'm hardly at a disadvantage. How I speak Spanish and English is a reflection of the culture I live every day. And unless there's something wrong about my almost bilingual and very bicultural life, then there's nothing wrong with combining the two languages I grew up with. Yo hablaré en dos idiomas as long as I can think in two (Figueroa, 2004, p. 286).

The classroom can generate discussions about *why* students think the author decided to write those particular words, phrases, or sentences in the other language. They are welcome to depict their opinions in the form of images, digitally, or through any other mode.

Translanguaging writing practices can be employed in order to leverage students' understanding of complex primary documents, such as *The Declaration of Independence*. This particular text is known for being very demanding in terms of language and complex in terms of content. In this particular lesson, outlined by Collins and Coie-Pena (2016), the teacher used BrainPop, which is an online and animated curricular content-based resource, to show a video of *The Declaration of Independence* in both Spanish and English before reading the text. In addition to the audio support, students were shown a painting of *The Declaration of Independence* taking place, as well as an image of the actual document. Students worked in groups and were given the printed text in English and Spanish. A questionnaire was distributed with questions written in English and translated in Spanish on the side as well as sentence frames in both languages to help students structure their written work. The lesson was conducted primarily in English. However, the history teacher ensured that all their students had access to the content and stimulated a learning environment fit for every student in that class, bilinguals and monolinguals alike.

IMPLICATIONS FOR LITERACY TEACHER EDUCATION

Bilingual/multilingual students bring a wealth of resources to the classroom (Griffin, Hemphill, Camp, & Wolf, 2004). Educators must acknowledge their funds of knowledge and constantly attempt to incorporate students' perspectives in the classroom, so the student is able to reach his/her fullest potential:

> For teachers, then, translanguaging is important not only because it allows them to engage each individual child holistically, but also because it is a way of differentiating instruction to ensure that all students are being cognitively, socially, and creatively challenged, while receiving the appropriate linguistic input and producing the adequate linguistic output in meaningful interactions and collaborative dialogue. (Garcia & Wei, 2013, p. 92)

Students whose native languages are maintained and supported in the classroom achieve greater academic success since their languages are reinforced both at home and at school (Nieto, 2009). A translanguaging pedagogy is important for bilingual/multilingual learners because it is built on their strengths as opposed to their limitations. It also helps students learn more meaningfully, reduce the risk of alienation, and sustain their language all at the same time (Garcia & Wei, 2013).

Contrary to what many teachers might think, tranglanguaging can be taught in any classroom scenario. Teachers should take the following five suggestions into consideration:

1. Bring to light the diversity in your classroom and engage in open dialogue with students. Bilingual/multilingual and monolingual students alike should be taught what it means to be multicultural citizens who respect and are knowledgeable of the many cultures that surround us. Engage students in conversations about diversity and explain why and for what purposes languages other than English are being included in translanguaging assignments in the classroom.

2. Get to know your students and their linguistic challenges. Translanguaging assignments encourage teachers to learn more about each student as individuals with different needs and contributions.

3. Teachers should identify translanguaging as a literacy device by allowing students to translate from their home-languages, engage with different modes, and produce texts that deal with identity. This in turn may motivate them to learn and they will see their language resources as strength and not a limitation.

4. Ask students for feedback on their experiences with translanguaging. It is important to identify students' feelings behind their translanguaging practices in order to ensure they are benefitting from it. If for some reason their skills are not evolving or they do not show signs that they are learning, it might be an indication that the assignment needs revision.

5. Make adjustments to materials you already possess. Translanguaging can be implemented in different classroom spaces and across subjects. Adapting assignments and incorporating translanguaging in monolingual assignments might be beneficial to bilinguals. (Kleyn, 2016, pp. 203–205)

REFLECTION QUESTIONS

1. Do you believe that there is a monolingual bias in school settings?
2. How can teachers who do not speak the language implement translanguaging activities? How can teachers address this possible issue?
3. How can teachers differentiate grades from monolingual students who wrote solely in English and from bilingual students who used translanguaging in their writing?
4. How can teachers assess students' work if they have no knowledge of some of their students' home languages?

REFERENCES

Bezemer, J., & Kress, G. (2008). Writing multimodal texts: A social semiotic account of designs teacher instructions. *Linguistics and Education, 19,* 166–178.

Blake, B. E. (2001). Fruit of the devil: Writing and English language learners. *Language Arts, 78*(5), 435–441.

Canagarajah, S. (2011). Codemeshing in academic writing: Identifying teachable strategies of translanguaging. *The Modern Language Journal*, *95*(3), 401–417.

Celic, C., & Seltzer, K. (2011). *Translanguaging: A CUNY-NYSIEB guide for educators.* New York, NY: CUNY-NYSIEB. Retrieved from http://www. nysieb. ws. gc. cuny. edu/files/2012/06/FINAL-Translanguaging-Guide-With-Cover-1. pdf.

Collins, B., & Coie-Peña, M. (2016). Navigating turbulent waters: Translanguaging to support academic and socioemotional well-being. In O. García & T. Kleyn (Eds.), *Translanguaging with multilingual students*. New York, NY: Routledge.

Creese, A., & Blackledge, A. (2010). Translanguaging in the bilingual classroom: A pedagogy for learning and teaching. *Modern Language Journal*, 94, 103–115.

Ebe, A. & Chapman-Santiago, C. (2016). *Student voices shining through: Exploring translanguaging as a literary device.* In O. García & T. Kleyn (Eds.), *Translanguaging with multilingual students*. New York, NY: Routledge

Figueroa, A. (2004). Speaking Spanglish. In Santa Ana, O. (2004). *Tongue-tied: The lives of multilingual children in public education*. Lanham, MD: Rowman & Littlefield.

Fu, D. (2009). *Writing between languages*. Portsmouth, NH: Heinemann.

García, O. (2009). *Bilingual education in the 21st century: A global perspective.* Malden, MA: Wiley/Blackwell.

Garcia, O., & Sylvan, C. E. (2011). Pedagogies and practices in multilingual classrooms: Singularities in pluralities. *The Modern Language Journal*, *95*(3), 385–400.

Garcia, O., & Wei, L. (2013). *Translanguaging: Language, bilingualism and education.* New York, NY: Palgrave Macmillan.

Ghiso, M. P., & Low, D. E. (2012). Students using multimodal literacies to surface micronarratives of United States immigration. *Literacy*, *47*(1), 26–34.

Gibson, W., & Brown, A. (2009). *Working with qualitative data*. London, UK: Sage.

Gort, M. (2006). Strategic codeswitching, interliteracy, and other phenomena of emergent bilingual writing: Lessons from first grade dual language classrooms. *Journal of Early Childhood Literacy*, *6*(3), 323–354. doi:10.1177/1468798406069796

Griffin, T. M., Hemphill, L., Camp, L., & Wolf, D. P. (2004). Oral discourse in the preschool years and later literacy development. *First Language*, *24*, 123–147.

Gutiérrez, R. (2007). Context matters: Equity, success, and the future of mathematics education. In T. Lamberg & L. R. Wiest (Eds.), *Proceedings of the 29th annual meeting of the North American Chapter of the International Group for the Psychology of Mathematics Education* (pp. 1–18). Reno, NV: University of Nevada.

Kabuto, B. (2010). *Becoming biliterate: Identity, ideology, and learning to read and write in two languages.* [AU: City, State:] Routledge.

Kleyn, T. (2016). Setting the path. In O. García & T. Kleyn (Eds.), *Translanguaging with multilingual students*. New York, NY: Routledge.

Kokkola, L. (2013). *Representing the Holocaust in children's literature*. Routledge.

Nichols, P. C., & Colon, M. (2000). Spanish literacy and the academic success of Latino high school students: Codeswitching as a classroom resource. *Foreign Language Annals*, *33*(5), 498–511.

Nieto, S. (2009). *Language, culture, and teaching: Critical perspectives*. New York, NY: Routledge.

Otheguy, R. (2016). Forward. In García, O., & Kleyn, T. (Eds.), *Translanguaging with multilingual students*. New York, NY: Routledge.

Pacheco, M. B., & Goodwin, A. P. (2013). Putting two and two together: Middle school students' morphological problem-solving strategies for unknown words. *Journal of Adolescent & Adult Literacy, 56*(7), 541–553.

Palmer, D. (2008). Diversity up close: Building alternative discourses in the dual immersion classroom. In T. Fortune & D. Tedick (Eds.), *Pathways in multilingualism: Evolving perspectives on immersion education* (pp. 97–116). London, UK: Multilingual Matters.

Razfar, A., & Gutiérrez, K. (2003). Reconceptualizing early childhood literacy: The sociocultural influence. *Handbook of early childhood literacy*, 34–47.

Sayer, P. (2013). Translanguaging, TexMex, and bilingual pedagogy: Emergent bilinguals learning through the vernacular. *TESOL Quarterly, 47*(1), 63–88.

Scott, V. M. (2008). What's the problem? L2 learners' use of the L1 during Consciousness-raising, form-focused tasks. *The Modern Language Journal, 92*(1), 100–113.

Sebba, M. (2012). Researching and theorizing multilingual texts' in M. Sebba (Ed.), *Language mixing and code-switching in writing: Approaches to mixed languages written discourse.* New York, NY: Longman.

Sfard, A., & Prusak, A. (2005). Telling identities: In search of an analytic tool for investigating learning as a culturally shaped activity. *Educational researcher, 34*(4), 14–22.

Smith, B. E. (2014). Beyond words: A review of research on adolescents and multimodal composition. In R. E. Ferdig & K. E. Pytash (Eds.). *Exploring multimodal composition and digital writing* (pp. 1–19). Hershey, PA: IGI Global.

Smith, B. E., Pacheco, M. B., & de Almeida, C. R. (2017). Multimodal codemeshing: Bilingual adolescents' processes composing across modes and languages. *Journal of Second Language Writing, 36*, 6–22.

Vygotsky, L. S. (1962). *Language and thought.* Ontario, Canada: Massachusetts Institute of Technology Press.

Woodley, H., & Brown, A. (2016). Balancing windows and mirrors: Translanguaging in a linguistically diverse classroom. In García, O., & Kleyn, T. (Eds.), *Translanguaging with multilingual students.* New York, NY: Routledge

CHAPTER 6

SCAFFOLDING MULTIMODAL COMPOSING IN THE MULTILINGUAL CLASSROOM

Blaine E. Smith and Daryl Axelrod

Along with helping to prepare today's students to navigate an increasingly networked and digital world, research emphasizes how integrating digital multimodal projects in the classroom can be particularly beneficial for bi/multilingual students. This chapter focuses on specific strategies for scaffolding multimodal composing in the multilingual classroom. First, we describe a multimodal framework and its key concepts. Next, we review the research literature on the main benefits of multimodal composing for bi/multilingual students, including increased engagement, multiple points of entry, opportunities for collaboration, and multimodal composing-to-learn. Finally, we suggest specific scaffolding strategies for supporting bi/multilingual learners' multimodal composing processes, as well as implications for teacher education.

Internationally, there have been shifts towards an expanded view of literacy that emphasizes the need for students to effectively communicate with multiple modes—including visuals, sound, text, and movement—in digital formats and online environments. Along with helping to prepare today's students to navigate an increasingly networked and digital world, research emphasizes how integrat-

Expanding Literacy Practices Across Multiple Modes and
Languages for Multilingual Students, pages 83–95.

ing digital multimodal projects (e.g., videos, podcasts, webpages, e-comics, multimodal PowerPoints, etc.) in the classroom can be particularly beneficial for bi/multilingual students. Multimodal composing offers numerous entry points for students to explore content and leverage their cultural lifeworlds in empowering ways (Anderson, Stewart, & Kachorsky, 2017; Honeyford, 2014; Hull, Stornaiuolo, & Sahni, 2010).

The goal of this chapter is to provide specific strategies for scaffolding multimodal composing in the multilingual classroom. First, we explain the multimodal framework and its key concepts. Second, we discuss four main benefits described in the research literature on multimodal composing and secondary bi/multilingual learners. Third, we suggest seven scaffolding strategies for integrating digital multimodal composing projects in the classroom. This chapter concludes with a discussion of implications for teacher education and reflection questions geared towards helping educators introduce multimodal projects within their own unique classroom contexts.

MULTIMODAL FRAMEWORK

Vital to a multimodal framework (Hodge & Kress, 1988; Kress, 2003, 2010) is the understanding that various modes—including linguistic, visual, audio, gestural, and spatial elements—are integral in all communication. When students design digital projects, they layer modes in unique ways to create complex and generative designs. According to this perspective, each mode in a composition is in dynamic interaction with other co-present modes and synergistically creates a new message (Kress, 2003, 2010). In other words, students' unique interweaving of different modes communicates messages that no single mode can express on its own (Jewitt, 2009).

An important concept of a multimodal framework involves examining the various ways modes can be combined—also referred to as *intersemiotic relationships.* There are infinite ways modes can be juxtaposed and/or layered, and composers must consider how different modes work together to create new multifaceted meanings. For example, corresponding modes in a digital project can align to emphasize a complementary message or diverge to create dissonance and convey different messages simultaneously (Unsworth, 2008).

A multimodal framework also emphasizes how visuals, sound, text, and movement offer unique communicative possibilities (Jewitt, 2009; Kress, 2010). These affordances of a mode -based on its social histories, cultural uses, and material features—offer potentials that make it well-suited for certain communicative tasks over other modes. Some multimodality research has examined how youth leveraged the affordances of specific modes in their digital products, including visuals (Shanahan, 2013), sounds (Wargo, 2017), colors (Pantaleo, 2012), and videos (Halverson, 2010). For example, an adolescent might be able to express personal emotions visually in a way that is not possible through linguistic modes whereas another student could prefer to rely on the stability and specificity of writing to convey their intended message. These modal affordances vary based on different composers, genres, and intended messages (Smith, 2017; Smith, Pacheco, & de Almeida 2017).

A multimodal framework broadens the communicative palette from which students can make meaning. They have a multitude of options for how different aspects of their digital projects are conveyed—through visuals, sound, text, or movement—and students must also consider how these modes build upon each other to convey a multifaceted message.

BENEFITS OF INTEGRATING DIGITAL MULTIMODAL COMPOSING IN THE MULTILINGUAL CLASSROOM

A growing body of research has examined the benefits of integrating digital multimodal composing into the multilingual classroom. In the following, we review literature in this area and present some of the main themes, including increased engagement, multiple points of entry, collaborative composing, and multimodal composing-to-learn.

Increased Engagement

Research describes how one of the key advantages of integrating multimodal composing projects in the multilingual classroom is increased engagement. A variety of reasons are attributed to students' motivation when communicating with digital tools and multiple modes.

First, many students enjoy being able to leverage their out-of-school digital literacies in the classroom (Pyo, 2016). Since an increasing majority of youth create and share digital projects outside of school, including digital videos, podcasts, and blogs (to name a few), students are excited when they have the opportunity to express their understanding through familiar and different digital genres (Ajayi, 2009; Clary, Kigotho, & Barros-Torning, 2013 Omerbasic, 2015; Toohey et al., 2015). For example, Newfield and D'abdon (2015) found that when students have "their own semiotic practices validated, participating in activities that appeal to and are meaningful to them, they are more likely to take responsibility for their learning and to participate actively in it" (p. 529). Another reason posited for why multimodal projects are engaging for bi/multilingual students is because they are often made public, distributed widely, and designed for authentic purposes (Black, 2008; Smith, 2014). Many teachers develop assignments that travel beyond their desk, intended to be shared with broad and receptive audiences (e.g., peers, community, and/or online) (Nordstrom, 2015). Finally, multimodal projects typically allow for students to make meaningful connections to their own lives and interests (Honeyford, 2014). Students delve into personally-relevant content (Danzak, 2011; DeBruin-Parecki, & Klein, 2003), make pop-culture connections (Black, 2008; Smith, 2018b) and explore social and political issues that matter to them (Chun, 2009; Pacheco & Smith, 2015; Smythe & Neufeld, 2010).

Multiple Points of Entry

Composing with multiple modes in digital environments offers bi/multilingual students multiple points of entry for engaging with content and constructing meaning (Jewitt, 2008). Research explains how the freedom of combining visuals, text, sound, and movement can create distinct opportunities for students to leverage their cultural and social capital, as well as express identities in empowering ways not typically afforded with written texts (Anderson, et al., 2017; Honeyford, 2014; Hull, Stornaiuolo, & Sahni, 2010). For example, Smythe & Neufeld (2010) examined how sixth and seventh grade emergent bilingual students from a range of countries (e.g., India, China, Afghanistan, and the Sudan) created podcasts where they told original stories through voice narration, sound effects, and music. They found that students drew from multiple semiotic resources, and that their unique background experiences and skills were assets during composing: "students usually known as struggling readers and writers were repositioned as historical and cultural subjects, knowledgeable and skilled in practices embedded in their transnational identities" (p. 492). Other research illuminates how bi/multilingual students often possess modal preferences for how they create their digital projects. Smith, Pacheco, and de Almeida (2017) found that there was variety in which modes bilingual adolescents preferred, and that students followed unique modal paths while composing. Some students launched into their process by working with visuals first, while other students created a written foundation before layering visuals or sound (Smith, Pacheco, & de Almeida, 2017). The multifaceted nature of multimodal composing processes allows for flexibility and individuality in how students chose to create their projects.

Collaborative Composing

A majority of studies that examine digital multimodal composing in secondary contexts illustrate it as a collaborative process with adolescents working in pairs or small groups. This research demonstrates how students work together on a wide range of multimodal projects throughout their composing process—including brainstorming ideas, composing with digital tools, editing, and presenting final products (Bruce, 2008; Smith, 2018a; Smith & de Oliveira, 2017; Wikan, Mølster, Faugli, & Hope, 2010). Research also illustrates how the multifaceted nature of multimodal projects allows for the distribution of tasks. Many times, students individually tackle a piece of a project and then collaborate with peers to integrate their contribution within the shared composition (Doering, Beach, & O'Brien, 2007; Smith, 2018a; Wikan, et al., 2010).

Students build upon each other's strengths (Beach & O'Brien, 2015), and often learn new technical and design skills from their peers while collaboratively composing (Pacheco & Smith, 2015). Research demonstrates how some students are able to step forward as "experts" and teach the class technical skills honed outside of school. For example, Oldaker (2010) described how student experts were viewed as vital resources when a seventh grade class created video games based on literature. As one student pointed out, "We had to ask a kid in our class that was already done with the game and knew a lot about it…he was very helpful. I don't know what the class would've done without him" (p. 22). Importantly, research emphasizes the "learner communities" developed through collaborative multimodal composing (Albers, 2006) have lasting impacts beyond specific projects to supporting bilingual students in achieving positive academic perspectives (Cummins, Hu, Markus, & Kristiina Montero, 2015).

Multimodal Composing-to-Learn

While research on multimodal composition in schools primarily focuses on the benefits for fostering student engagement, identity expression, and collaboration, recent research has focused on how multimodal composing can also support academic learning (Early & Marshall, 2008; Bailey, 2009; Smith, 2018). Similar to scholarship on writing-to-learn, which explores how writing serves as a tool for thinking, developing research examines *multimodal composing-to-learn*. That is, understanding how composing through multiple modes supports and possibly transcends learning.

Across different content areas, studies illustrate how students demonstrate a deeper understanding of concepts through digital multimodal composing. Some research in secondary STEM classrooms emphasizes the importance of multiple representations, which include visuals and text, for promoting conceptual learning (Ainsworth, 1999). Gunel, Hand, and Gunduz (2006) found that students gained a deeper understanding of physics concepts by creating a multimodal presentation compared to writing a summary report. Within the instructional context of secondary English Language Arts, research has examined multimodal literary analysis (Doering et al., 2007; Pacheco & Smith, 2015; Smith, 2018). Jocius (2013) described how twelfth grade students learned literary devices through creating digital videos and multimodal PowerPoint presentations. Similarly, Bailey (2009) illustrated how ninth grade students "learned literary elements, poetic devices, rhetorical elements, and used reading and writing strategies in ways that previous classes never had before" through multimodal projects connected to literature (p. 230). Finally, some research illustrates how multimodal projects support the learning of specific academic vocabulary (Kuo, Yu, & Hsiao, 2013; Stille & Prasad, 2015). This research elucidates how representing vocabulary through multiple modes can be beneficial for bi/multilingual students (Amicucci & Lassiter, 2014).

EXPANDING LITERACY PRACTICES: CLASSROOM STRATEGIES

While research emphasizes the various benefits for integrating multimodal composing in multilingual classrooms, it is important that students receive support when creating with digital tools. In the following, we present different strategies for scaffolding students' multimodal composing processes.

Explicitly Teaching Multimodality Concepts and Vocabulary

Since most classrooms represent a wide variety of students with technology experience—ranging from little to no access at home, to primarily using digital tools for socializing purposes, and skilled students who share their own multimodal creations online—it's important for teachers to provide explicit instruction so that all students are placed on even footing. First, students should learn about the concept of *multimodality*. This includes helping students become familiar with what constitutes different *modes* (e.g., visuals, sound, text, movement, and gesture) and how they can be used for various communicative purposes. Multimodal analysis activities at the beginning of a unit can support students to develop an understanding of these key concepts. For example, teachers can present a short video example that incorporates a variety of visuals, sounds (e.g., music, sound effects, speech), movement, and text. Next, provide students with a graphic organizer that clearly delineates different modes into separate categories. Continue with several viewings of the video where the class focuses on one specific mode at a time (e.g., movement). Students can brainstorm and discuss how that specific mode is used to communicate in the video, as well as the unique benefits it contains for making meaning. After each focused viewing, students can also discuss how each mode works together to create the overall message of the video.

Another activity that helps students to understand the communicative power of different modes involves showing mash-up videos. For example, students can watch a short clip from a movie (e.g., a scene from Disney's *Lion King*) and discuss how they see the music contributing to the action and tone of the clip. There are a variety of these mash-ups on YouTube that repeatedly show a scene with different music and sound effects (e.g., https://www.youtube.com/watch?v=ecYgqLml89c). Next, show the exact same clip but with dissimilar background music, ranging from happy to spooky to melancholic, and discuss how a message can completely change by modal variations. Activities like these are engaging for students and allow them to delve into multimodality concepts.

Providing Explicit Technical Mini-Lessons

It is also imperative for students to receive needed technical instruction about the digital tools (Dalton, 2013; Mills, 2010). Instead of engaging in one long technical tutorial at the beginning of a multimodal composing unit, we find it is more effective to provide short, targeted technical mini-lessons across several sessions so that students do not feel overwhelmed. Tutorials at the beginning of the unit should cover basic functions of the digital tools to be used, and over time students should experience more advanced tutorials that correlate with their progress and interests.

Importantly, teachers should not feel like they have to shoulder all of the technical instruction for the class. Especially for the less tech-savvy teachers, they should leverage the wealth of technical resources surrounding them to support students during the composing process. For example, YouTube and other websites have many short videos that cover specific technical skills that can be shared with a class. Students should also learn how to proactively access the technical support they need when they need it. We find it effective to provide students with a list of resources or links they can individually reference as they compose.

While it is important for teachers to be familiar with the technology themselves, allowing students to take the role of expert from time to time is not only a lifesaver when your technical expertise reaches its limits but also develops a collaborative workshop environment where students can leverage their outside interests and skills in the classroom. Use surveys or other means to learn about students' interests and plan ahead for a few students to lead mini-lessons, or help students become comfortable standing up for impromptu sharing sessions about techniques they already know or just discovered through experimentation. These student "experts" can also serve as valuable resources for peers during composing sessions.

Providing Models and Demonstrating the Composing Process

The possibilities for what students can create through multiple modes broadens when they are able to see a variety of peer and real-world examples. Teachers can show an array of examples at the beginning of their unit and have students reflect upon how different modes were used and their effectiveness. These examples will spark students' imaginations and allow them to emulate and build upon what they see.

When asking students to develop a digital product with unfamiliar technology, it is also wise for teachers to attempt the project themselves first. Creating multimodal projects creates three important instructional advantages. First, it familiarizes teachers with the technology and allows them to discover potential stumbling blocks ahead of students and learn how to resolve them. Second, teachers can provide a think-aloud of their composing process and why they made certain design decisions. Third, if they do not have previous student work to use as exemplars, it can provide a model for students, who may have difficulty conceptualizing the finished product. It often works well to leave an example incomplete to actively model aspects of the process in class and incorporate student suggestions and feedback. This not only helps students understand the process, but also the technical and creative considerations a designer could make (Dalton, 2013).

Fostering Collaboration and Peer Feedback

As demonstrated by research, multimodal projects lend themselves well to collaboration. Students work together throughout the process to problem solve, provide feedback to one another, and share their unique skills and perspectives. Multimodal projects are often multi-part and involve different types of digital tools. It's advantageous to let students collaborate so they can divide the labor based on the physical technology, different modalities, sections of the content, and/or personal skills and interests (Smith & de Oliveira, 2017).

Similar to writing workshops, peer feedback is also essential for productive multimodal composing. Set aside time for students to share their in-process work through informal presentations or gallery-walks. Students can also participate in peer workshops and class showcases at the end of a unit. In accord with multi-modal literacies research, it is also beneficial for students to share their projects with authentic audiences (Black, 2008). Teachers can post students' work on a class webpage or find real-world venues for others to engage with their composi-tions.

Asking Students to Reflect on their Process and Final Product

Along with providing opportunities for students to informally and formally share their work, it is essential to have them submit reflections with their mul-timodal compositions. In these assignments, students can address specific ques-tions aimed at uncovering their process, design decisions, and connections to the content. Not only are these reflections an important part of the learning and com-posing process (Bransford, Brown, & Cocking, 2000), but they can better illumi-nate student thinking, purposeful rhetorical decisions, and complex use of modes.

Students can also create digital reflections (Smith & Dalton, 2016) through a variety of multimodal means, including digital video, podcasts, and online com-ics. Multimodal reflections allow for students to leverage the digital tools they learned in class and offer unique introspective space for students to uncover their collaborative processes and views on their experiences. They also provided a low-stakes opportunity for students to continue learning the new tools and gain ex-perience with multimodal composing. In addition to fostering a meta-awareness of their multimodal composing processes, these reflections served as insightful formative assessments for the teacher.

Allowing Freedom in Composing Process and Use of Digital Tools

Along with supporting students' processes with the various scaffolds dis-cussed, it's imperative to also allow for flexibility and individualism in students' multimodal composing processes. Research demonstrates how adolescents often exhibit unique modal preferences (Kress, 2010; Smith, 2017), relying on modes (e.g., visuals, sound, text, movement) in different ways to make meaning. As such, students' processes should not be stifled by having to follow a regimented step-by-step order for completing their projects, or forced to write before attending to non-linguistic modes. Some students might prefer to brainstorm through search-ing for visuals or remixing sounds before they write. It is also beneficial to allow students freedom in the types of digital tools they leverage during their compos-ing process. Teachers should provide options for different types of technology and resources students can use, and let them follow their own unique composing paths. Striking this delicate balance between scaffolding the multimodal composing process while also fostering creative individuality will support students in making the most of the multiple entry points and unique meaning-making offered through digital projects.

Preparing for Roadblocks

Finally, it is extremely important to plan for technological roadblocks of all kinds when integrating multimodal projects. Teachers can model resourcefulness for students by treating roadblocks as learning moments, and prepare to minimize them by considering a few logistical questions. Plan for pointing students to find public domain images, music clips, and sound effects. When possible, provide override access for potentially blocked sites such as Google Images and YouTube, and if that is not possible, plan to provide a set of pre-approved media resources. To avoid lost work, prearrange cloud storage or access to flash drives and require students to save frequently and in multiple locations. Roadblocks are bound to occur when introducing technology in the classroom; however, they can be minimized through strategic planning, a positive outlook, and adaptive thinking.

IMPLICATIONS FOR LITERACY TEACHER EDUCATION

In order for pre-service teachers to understand the benefits and learning possibilities of multimodal composing, they need to gain first-hand experience themselves. Teacher educators should incorporate the concept of *multimodality* and teaching pre-service teachers, including what constitutes different *modes* (e.g., visuals, sound, text, movement, and gesture) and how they can be used for different communicative purposes. Preservice teachers can participate in many of the scaffolding strategies previously described to learn these concepts, including focused analyses and examining an array of digital examples. Developing multimodal projects can help teachers gain hands-on experience with strategically combining multiple modes for different communicative effects. These multimodal projects will also allow preservice teachers to have examples they can use if assigning a similar multimodal project with their future students.

The same way that students should receive needed technical instruction about digital tools, it is necessary for teachers to understand the tools that they will use with their future students. Our recommendation is to provide short, targeted technical mini-lessons as mentor activities for teachers across a specific course that will focus on multimodal literacies. Pre-service teachers will be more likely to integrate digital multimodal projects if they feel comfortable using different digital tools.

Another opportunity for teacher education is to foster collaboration for pre-service teachers. Because multimodal projects typically involve multiple parts and different types of digital tools, teacher educators can create collaborative projects so pre-service teachers can work together to divide work, learn the digital tools, and share their unique skills and perspectives. Pre-service teachers should also reflect on their process and final product and consider ways to integrate multimodal composing into their future classrooms.

REFLECTION QUESTIONS

This chapter discussed a multimodality framework, key themes in the research literature, and scaffolding strategies for integrating digital multimodal composing in the multilingual classroom. Below are some reflection questions to consider for supporting your unique students' multimodal composing processes within your specific instructional context.

1. How can some of your traditional written assignments be transformed into a digital multimodal project?
2. How can the key concepts you want students to learn be expressed through different modalities?
3. How can you create opportunities for your students to leverage their unique skills and cultural lifeworlds through digital multimodal composing?
4. What are some ways students can create multimodal projects for authentic purposes and audiences in your classroom?
5. How should your assessments be adapted when assigning multimodal projects?

REFERENCES

Ainsworth, S. (1999). The functions of multiple representations. *Computers & Education, 33*(2–3), 131–152.

Ajayi, L. (2009). English as a second language learners' exploration of multimodal texts in a junior high school. *Journal of Adolescent & Adult Literacy, 52*(7), 585–595. doi:10.1598/JAAL.52.7.4

Albers, P. (2006). Imagining the possibilities in multimodal curriculum design. *English Education*, 75–101.

Amicucci, A. N., & Lassiter, T. (2014). Multimodal concept drawings: Engaging EAL learners in brainstorming about course terms. *TESOL Journal, 5*(3), 523–531. doi:10.1002/tesj.161

Anderson, K. T., Stewart, O. G., & Kachorsky, S. D. (2017). Seeing academically marginalized students' multimodal designs from a position of strength. *Written Communication, 34*(2), 104–134.

Bailey, N. M. (2009). "It makes it more real": Teaching new literacies in a secondary English classroom. *English Education, 41*(3), 207–234.

Beach, R. & O'Brien, D. (2015). Fostering students' science inquiry through app affordances of multimodality, collaboration, interactivity, and connectivity. *Reading & Writing Quarterly, 31*(2), 119–134.

Black, R. W. (2008). *Adolescents and online fanfiction.* New York, NY: Peter Lang.

Bransford, J. D., Brown A. L., & Cocking R. R. (2000). *How people learn: Brain, mind, experience, and school.* Washington, DC: National Academy Press.

Bruce, D. (2008). Visualizing literacy: Building bridges with media. *Reading & Writing Quarterly, 24*(3), 264–282.

Chun, C. W. (2009). Critical literacies and graphic novels for English-Language Learners: Teaching Maus. *Journal of Adolescent & Adult Literacy, 53*(2), 144–153.

Clary, D., Kigotho, M., & Barros-Torning, M. (2013). Harnessing mobile technologies to enrich adolescents' multimodal literacy practices in middle years classrooms. *Literacy Learning: The Middle Years, 21*(3), 49–60.

Cummins, J., Hu, S., Markus, P., & Kristiina Montero, M. (2015). Identity texts and academic achievement: Connecting the dots in multilingual school contexts. *TESOL Quarterly, 49*(3), 555–581. doi:10.1002/tesq.241

Dalton, B. (2013). Multimodal composition and the Common Core State Standards. *The Reading Teacher, 66*(4), 333–339.

Danzak, R. (2011). Defining identities through multiliteracies: EL teens narrate their immigration experiences as graphic stories. *Journal of Adolescent & Adult Literacy, 55*(3), 187–196.

DeBruin-Parecki, A., & Klein, H. A. (2003). Stvaranje Prijatelja/Making friends: Multimodal literacy activities as bridges to intercultural friendship and understanding. *Journal of Adolescent & Adult Literacy, 46*(6), 506–13.

Doering, A., Beach, R., & O'Brien, D. (2007). Infusing multimodal tools and digital literacies into an English education program. *English Education, 40*(1), 41–60.

Early, M., & Marshall, S. (2008). Adolescent ESL students' interpretation and appreciation of literary texts: A case study of multimodality. *Canadian Modern Language Review, 64*(3), 377–397.

Gunel, M., Hand, B., & Gunduz, S. (2006). Comparing student understanding of quantum physics when embedding multimodal representations into two different writing formats: Presentation format versus summary report format. *Science Education, 10,* 1093–1112.

Halverson, E. R. (2010). Film as identity exploration: A multimodal analysis of youth-produced films. *Teachers College Record, 112*(9), 2352–2378.

Hodge, R. I. V. & Kress, G. (1988). *Social semiotics.* Cambridge: Polity Press.

Honeyford, M. A. (2014). From aquí and allá: Symbolic convergence in the multimodal literacy practices of adolescent immigrant students. *Journal of Literacy Research, 46*(2), 194–233. doi:10.1177/1086296X14534180

Hull, G. A., Stornaiuolo, A., & Sahni, U. (2010). Cultural citizenship and cosmopolitan practice: Global youth communicate online. *English Education, 42*(4), 331–367.

Jewitt, C. (2008). Multimodality and literacy in school classrooms. *Review of Research in Education, 32*(1), 241–267.

Jewitt, C. (Ed.). (2009). *The Routledge handbook of multimodal analysis.* New York, NY: Routledge.

Jocius, R. (2013). Exploring adolescents' multimodal responses to "The Kite Runner": Understanding how students use digital media for academic purposes. *Journal of Media Literacy Education, 5*(1), 310–325.

Kress, G. (2003). *Literacy in the new media age.* London, UK: Routledge.

Kress, G. (2010). *Multimodality: A social semiotic approach to contemporary communication.* New York, NY: Routledge

Kuo, F., Yu, P., & Hsiao, W. (2013). Develop and evaluate the effects of multimodal presentation system on elementary ESL students. *TOJET : The Turkish Online Journal of Educational Technology*, *12*(4) [AU: page range]

Mills, K. A. (2010). Shrek meets Vygotsky: Rethinking adolescents' multimodal literacy practices in schools. *Journal of Adolescent & Adult Literacy*, *54*(1), 35–45.

Newfield, D., & D'abdon, R. (2015). Reconceptualising poetry as a multimodal genre. *TESOL Quarterly*, *49*(3), 510–532. doi:10.1002/tesq.239

Nordstrom, J. (2015). Flexible bilingualism through multimodal practices: Studying K–12 community languages online. *International Journal of Bilingual Education and Bilingualism*, *18*(4), 395–408.

Oldaker, A. (2010). Creating video games in middle school language arts classroom: A narrative account. *Voices from the Middle, 17*(3), 19–26.

Omerbasic, D. (2015). Literacy as a translocal practice: Digital multimodal literacy practices among girls resettled as refugees. *Journal of Adolescent & Adult Literacy*, *58*(6), 472. doi:10.1002/jaal.389

Pacheco, M. B., & Smith, B. E. (2015). Across languages, modes, and identities: Bilingual adolescents' multimodal codemeshing in the literacy classroom. *Bilingual Research Journal*, *38*(3), 292–312.

Pantaleo, S. (2012). Meaning-making with colour in multimodal texts: An 11-year-old student's purposeful 'doing.' *Literacy, 46*(3), 147–155.

Pyo, J. (2016). Bridging in-school and out-of-school literacies: An adolescent EL's composition of a multimodal project. *Journal of Adolescent & Adult Literacy, 59*(4), 421–430.

Shanahan, L. E. (2013). Composing "kid-friendly" multimodal text: When conversations, instruction, and signs come together. *Written Communication, 30*(2), 194–227.

Smith, B. E. (2014). Beyond words: A review of research on adolescents and multimodal composition. In R. E. Ferdig & K. E. Pytash (Eds.), *Exploring multimodal composition and digital writing* (pp. 1–19). Hershey, PA: IGI Global.

Smith, B. E. (2017). Composing across modes: A comparative analysis of adolescents' multimodal composing processes. *Learning, Media & Technology, 42*(3), 259–278.

Smith, B. E. (2018). Composing for affect, audience, and identity: Toward a multidimensional understanding of adolescents' multimodal composing goals and designs. *Written Communication, 35*(2), 182–214.

Smith, B. E. & Dalton, B. (2016). "Seeing it from a different light": Adolescents' video reflections about their multimodal compositions. *Journal of Adolescent & Adult Literacy, 59*(6), 719–729.

Smith, B. E., & de Oliveira, L. C. (2017). English language learners' collaboration through multimodal composition. In M. Dantas-Whitney, & S. Rilling. (Eds.). *TESOL voices: Secondary education.* Alexandria, VA: TESOL Press.

Smith, B. E., Pacheco, M. B., & de Almeida, C. R. (2017). Multimodal codemeshing: Bilingual adolescents' processes composing across modes and languages. *Journal of Second Language Writing, 36,* 6–22.

Smythe, S., & Neufeld, P. (2010). "Podcast time": Negotiating digital literacies and communities of learning in a middle years ELL classroom. *Journal of Adolescent & Adult Literacy, 53*(6), 488–496.

Stille, S., & Prasad, G. (2015). "Imaginings": Reflections on plurilingual students' creative multimodal works. *TESOL Quarterly, 49*(3), 608–621. doi:10.1002/tesq.240

Toohey, K., Dagenais, D., Fodor, A., Hof, L., Nuñez, O., Singh, A., & Schulze, L. (2015). "That sounds so cooool": Entanglements of children, digital tools, and literacy practices. *TESOL Quarterly, 49*(3), 461–485. doi:10.1002/tesq.236

Unsworth, L. (2008). Multiliteracies and metalanguage: Describing image/text relations as a resource for negotiating multimodal texts. In J. Coiro, M. Knobel, C. Lankshear, & D.J. Leu (Eds.), *Handbook of research on new literacies* (pp. 377–405). New York, NY: Lawrence Erlbaum Associates.

Wargo, J. M. (2017). Rhythmic rituals and emergent listening: Intra-activity, sonic sounds and digital composing with young children. *Journal of Early Childhood Literacy, 17*(3), 392–408.

Wikan, G., Mølster, T., Faugli, B., & Hope, R. (2010). Digital multimodal texts and their role in project work: Opportunities and dilemmas. *Technology, Pedagogy and Education, 19*(2), 225–235.

CHAPTER 7

WRITING FOR SOCIAL JUSTICE

A Promising Practice for Culturally and Linguistically Diverse Adolescents

Kristin Kibler

This chapter reviews the literature on social justice writing projects for culturally and linguistically diverse adolescents and provides recommendations for practitioners. Since social justice education is meant to challenge and counter misconceptions and stereotypes that lead to structural inequality and discrimination, the chapter highlights ways to provide students with resources to reach their full learning potential, build on each student's talents and strengths, and create a learning environment that promotes critical thinking and increases student agency for social change.

Social justice "is a way of approaching public education, and teacher education, that ensures that it will be as open and equitable as possible to all children regardless of their identities, biologies, or experiences" (Alsup & Miller, 2014, p. 199). To ensure that secondary English language arts (ELA) teachers can utilize social justice approaches in the current era of testing accountablity, the National Council of Teachers of English (NCTE) adopted a new social justice standard for initial teacher preparation (Alsup & Miller, 2014). Standard VI requires candidates to "demonstrate knowledge of how theories and research about social jus-

Expanding Literacy Practices Across Multiple Modes and
Languages for Multilingual Students, pages 97–111.
Copyright © 2019 by Information Age Publishing
All rights of reproduction in any form reserved.

tice, diversity, equity, student identities, and schools as institutions can enhance students' opportunities to learn in English Language Arts" (NCTE, 2012, p. 1).

Although social justice is critical in ELA, its four components can be used in any subject area with any students: countering misconceptions and stereotypes that lead to structural inequality and discrimination, providing all students with the resources to reach their full academic potential, building on each student's talents, strengths, language, and experiences, and creating a learning environment that augments critical thinking and agency for social change (Nieto & Bode, 2008). Writing provides an excellent medium for bringing these social justice components into the classroom, but it is not clear what this looks like in practice. This is particularly true in the age of high-stakes testing, where many pacing guides and program curricula offer little flexibility.

This chapter is based upon a review of the academic literature about culturally and linguistically diverse (CLD) adolescents writing for social justice. The review examined the theoretical frameworks of the writing projects, the different types of projects, and the project outcomes. I will provide findings from the literature review as well as examples of social justice approaches to writing that have been successfully utilized with different groups of CLD adolescents. Implications for teacher education will also be discussed.

THEORETICAL FRAMEWORK

There are two predominant theoretical frameworks guiding the area of CLD students writing for social justice: culturally relevant pedagogy (Ladson-Billings, 1995) and critical literacy (Freire, 1970). These theoretical lenses fit under the umbrella of multicultural education and work well in conjunction. In fact, critical literacy can be viewed as a way of making sense of and utilizing culturally relevant pedagogy in the classroom (Lopez, 2011).

The term "critical literacy" became known to a wide audience through Paulo Freire's seminal book titled *Pedagogy of the Oppressed*. Freire (1970) believed that traditional educational systems treated students as empty "containers" to be filled and called this concept "banking." Freire (1970) rejected banking and other traditional teaching techniques that passed on dominant societal narratives and often required rote memorization. Critical literacy was presented as the solution as it requires questioning the social, political, and economic contexts within which the text being examined was written (Freire, 1970). In academic settings, students must be active and reflective as they read texts through a critical literacy lens in order to better understand issues of power, inequality, and injustice (Coffey, 2011). By analyzing texts and media in this manner, CLD students can examine how cultures and identities are represented or misrepresented (Lopez, 2011).

Culturally relevant pedagogy is concerned with increasing student achievement, helping students accept and affirm their cultural identities, and teaching students to critically view and challenge inequities in their schools and communities (Ladson-Billings, 1995). Although Ladson-Billings (1995) was studying effective teachers of African American students when she created this theoretical model, she noted that "issues of culturally relevant teaching can and should be considered cross-culturally" (p. 484). In practice, culturally relevant pedagogy places the cultures, languages, and experiences of CLD students at the center of classroom instruction to increase engagement and academic achievement (Lopez, 2011).

SOCIAL JUSTICE WRITING PROJECTS

Of the eighteen articles that the literature search yielded, the majority of them described social justice writing projects that were carried out in urban classrooms. The other projects were also carried out in urban areas, but took place in settings such as after school and summer school programs. The out-of-school projects tended to be for a specific group (e.g. Latinas, African American males or females, refugee students).

As Table 7.1 shows, the majority of the writing projects were multi-genre. One example of this is a workshop in which ninth grade students composed poems, narratives, and expositions about issues that were personally, socially, and politically important to them (Chapman, Hobbel, & Alvarado, 2011). The unit began by asking the following questions: "What concerns you? Which of these issues concerns your families and communities? Do these same issues distress the world on a global level?" (Chapman et al., 2011, p. 540). The students' responses generated topics that the teacher could build upon and make connections to. Some of the students had immigrated to the United States and were able to talk about issues from other parts of the world as well as issues in their new community. This workshop

TABLE 7.1. Types of Social Justice Writing Projects

Written Products	n
Multi-genre (e.g. poetry plus narratives)	8
Narratives	7
Performance Poetry/Spoken Word	4
Poetry	3
Multimodal	3
Auto-Ethnographic Narratives	2
Critical Reflections	2
Short Stories	2
Counternarratives	1
Reading Responses	1
Letters	1

*Some of the projects included more than one product and were therefore double coded

used small peer-review groups in which the students provided statements of affirmation, solidarity, and critique (see Chapman et al., 2011).

Another example also comes from a diverse 9th grade classroom (Singer & Shagoury, 2005). This project required students to read, discuss, and write across multiple genres: poetry, narratives, persuasive, imaginative, and expository. The teacher wove the theme of social activism throughout her year-long global literature curriculum, which included stories about groups in the United States that have historically been marginalized. Each text, project, and writing skills/social activism workshop throughout the year was designed to lead up to the final unit on social activism (see Singer & Shagoury, 2005), which began with the students selecting a biography or autobiography about an activist. The capstone was an activism gallery in which students showcased their narratives, poems, artwork, music, and so forth.

Themes from Project Outcomes

All of the reviewed articles listed more than one outcome from the social justice writing projects, whether they were explicitly stated, implied, or a combination of both. There is some overlap in the project outcome themes and all of them work well together. Table 7.2 depicts the top five themes from the project outcomes. These are briefly discussed below in order to show some of the potential benefits of CLD students writing for social justice.

The primary outcome that was mentioned in the articles was increased social consciousness (Camangian, 2008; DeJaynes, 2015; Garcia et al., 2015; Jocson, 2009; McCarther & Davis, 2015; Miller, 2014; Ramirez & Jimenez-Silva, 2015; Seher, 2011; Singer & Shagoury, 2005; Tatum & Gue, 2012; Wissman, 2011). A few different terms were included in this theme such as increased civic consciousness, increased civic engagement, social transformation agency, advocating for social justice, and community empowerment. Regardless of the utilized term, the result was an increased awareness of inequities in the students' personal experiences, community, nation, etc. As a result of this heightened awareness, the students were more empowered to work towards equity and social justice.

TABLE 7.2. Project Outcome Themes

Project Outcome Themes	n
Increased Social Consciousness	11
Increased Critical Literacy Skills	10
Developed Voice	9
Negotiated Identities	7
Ability to Produce Counternarratives	5

*Some of the projects reported more than one outcome and were therefore double coded

The outcome of increased critical literacy skills was reported almost as frequently as increased social consciousness. The majority of the articles stated that the students were better able to think critically about texts and/or media and in tandem were better able to read and write critically (Carmangian, 2008; Chapman et al., 2011; DeJaynes, 2015; Garcia & Gaddes, 2012; Jocson, 2009; McCarther & Davis, 2015; Muhammed & McArthur, 2015, Ramirez & Jiminez-Silva, 2015; Scarbrough & Allen, 2014; Singer & Shagoury, 2005).

The third most prevalent theme was development of voice (Carmangian, 2008; DeJaynes, 2015; Garcia et al., 2015; Muhammad & McArthur, 2015; Ramirez & Jiminez-Silva, 2015); Scarbrough & Allen, 2014; Seher, 2011; Singer & Shagoury, 2005; Stewart, 2015). In writing, voice means making a composition one's own. Mariconda (2015) defines voice as a unique style, quality, or tone that makes writing stand out. In social justice writing, student voice often means student input, typically regarding issues of equity.

The next prevalent them was negotiated identities and identity shifts. These were reported in projects where students critically read and wrote about texts that they saw themselves reflected in (DeJaynes, 2015; Garcia & Gaddes, 2012; Muhammed & McArthur, 2015; Ramirez & Jiminez-Silva, 2015; Stewart, 2015; Tatum & Gue, 2012; Wissman, 2011). Gee (2000) states that "when any human being acts and interacts in a given context, others recognize that person as acting as a certain 'kind of person' or even as several different 'kinds' at once (p. 99). Gee (2000) goes on to define identity as "being recognized as a certain 'kind of person' in a given context" (p. 99).

Finally, the students were able not only to recognize dominant narratives in the texts and/or the media, but that the projects enabled them to write narratives that went against that (Carmagian, 2008; DeJaynes, 2015; Garcia et al., 2015; Muhammed & McArthur, 2015; Wissman, 2011). These are commonly known as counternarratives.

CLASSROOM APPLICATIONS

As the themes from the project outcomes demonstrate, writing is an excellent way to address Nieto and Bode's (2008) aforementioned social justice components while also improving literacy skills. The students were able to produce counternarratives against common misconceptions and stereotypes, their improved critical literacy and critical thinking skills will help them reach their full learning potential, and their increased voice, social consciousness, and negotiated identities better prepares them to be agents of social change. To obtain similar outcomes, keep in mind the importance of building upon each student's strengths, experiences, and language (Nieto & Bode, 2008), raising the students' awareness about issues that affect themselves and/or their families and community, affirming their identities, creating a sense of solidarity among the students, supporting them in receiving and implementing critical feedback, and having authentic audiences for sharing their final work (Chapman et al., 2011).

The section below highlights examples of social justice writing projects from the top three kinds of texts: narratives, performance poetry, and multimodal texts. Although some projects were carried out in classrooms and others in outside of school programs, they demonstrate different ways that social justice writing can be used in different settings with different groups of CLD adolescents. Strategies are embedded within the projects, including allowing the emergent bilingual students to translanguage, or use "their full linguistic repertoire" in their planning and in their compositions (Otheguy, García, & Reid, 2015, p. 283). In other words, they were allowed to use their home languages and were not limited by English only.

Narratives

Narratives were the most common type of written product across the projects. This genre can be defined as any type of writing that tells a story (e.g. biographies, autobiographies, short stories, novels). Although narratives can be fiction or non-fiction, the latter was used for social justice writing. Narratives are quite versatile and can be a useful tool in writing for social justice. The projects that are highlighted below show the use of social justice narratives with refugee students, within a required unit in an 11th grade urban classroom, and with African American females writing against how they are portrayed by the media.

Migration Narratives. The first example is Stewart's (2015) use of migration narratives with 9th and 10th grade refugees, most of whom came from Myanmar. This teacher/researcher led a summer school session in which the participants read about different refugee experiences and then wrote their personal narratives about immigrating to the United States. Three texts were selected for shared reading and the students chose other books for their free reading time. The readings were carefully selected in order to be accessible and to reflect the students' experiences and backgrounds. They provided a basis for discussions and writing. Stewart (2015) used a writer's workshop model as well as individual conferencing to provide extra writing support. The students worked together to discuss what they wanted to say in their first language, to select the correct English terms, and to revise and edit their work.

Stewart (2015) was very intentional about learning from the students' responses to the literature and their narratives in order to co-construct knowledge along with them, to learn from them, and to improve her teaching. This is an important social justice-oriented approach as refugee students often have had limited or interrupted formal education and are frequently viewed through a deficit lens of the things they cannot do rather than the things that they can. It also places the students at the center of instruction and builds upon their funds of knowledge (González, Moll, & Amanti, 2005), or linguistic and cultural resources. "Culturally and linguistically diverse students' funds of knowledge are deep and often vary greatly from our own, providing a space for them to teach us, to share with us experiences that we do not have" (Stewart, 2015, p. 157).

Projects such as this have potential for undocumented and unaccompanied youth as well as student with refugee status, since "sharing one's life story, particularly the stories of immigrant or refugee students, may have a far greater impact than improving English-language literacy skills" (Stewart, 2015, p. 152). It also holds potential for a wide range of emergent bilinguals who can share their life, immigration, and acculturation stories.

Personal War Stories. These narratives were composed by 11th grade students in a New York City school (Seher, 2011) in conjunction with a unit on a Vietnam War novel where the students were required to read *The Things They Carried* (O'Brien, 1990). The teacher adapted this unit and integrated social justice writing after a student felt that he was unfairly suspended and after the students' reactions to the novel fell flat. Seher (2011) saw a connection between the suspended student's sense of powerlessness and the protagonist's powerlessness in the novel and reworked the remainder of the unit so that the students could analyze resistance to perceived injustice during the Vietnam War and in their own lives.

In order to learn about resistance to the war, Seher (2011) showed a documentary about Bill Ayers and his role in the Weather Underground. "In contrast to O'Brien's soldiers, Ayers organized during the same era to challenge a war and political system that he believed was unjust. Ayers had grappled with the question of resistance versus compliance in a very real way" (Seher, 2011, p. 171). She was inspired by Freire's (1970) problem-posing education, where "the teacher poses problems and presents material based on 'generative themes'—themes that students themselves identify as relevant to their lives through dialogue with one another and the teacher" (p. 180). She therefore reframed the unit around the students' questions and experiences/generative themes. Stories about Bill Ayer's resistance to the war served as the basis for examining the complexities of resistance, values, right and wrong, and injustice. The students were able to discuss this with Mr. Ayers via a video call and also in person since he agreed to visit their class. All of this ultimately went into the student's personal "war stories," in which they wrote about injustices and their resistance to them (Seher, 2011).

Counternarratives. The final example is one of counternarratives, or writing against the dominant narratives in a society. In this case, eight African American female teenagers wrote to disrupt how they were portrayed in the media (Muhammad & McArthur, 2015). This occurred during a summer writing institute that was held with the following intent: "to move toward a horizon of providing Black girls the space needed to not only make sense of the representations available through media outlets but also provide spaces to accept, resist, reorient, or negotiate such depictions as they develop identity" (Muhammad & McArthur, 2015, p. 135). The participants were asked the following questions in a pre-workshop interview: "Based on your experiences, how are African American women and girls portrayed in media such as music, television, Internet, magazine, and radio? Why do you think African American women and girls are portrayed in these ways?" (Muhammad & McArthur, 2015, p. 136). The girls' responses indicated that they felt judged by their hair, were depicted as loud, angry, and violent, and that they were often sexualized and objectified (Muhammad & McArthur, 2015). Importantly, "We found that the ways the girls desired to be represented (as evident by their self-descriptions) were in opposition to the ways they felt society and media viewed them" (Muhammad & McArthur, 2015, p. 138).

Although the participants also wrote poetry, short stories, essays, and letters, the counternarratives are at the heart of this project. Using this approach, students can "examine and interrogate media images and depictions of diverse groups in society" (Muhammad & McArthur, 2015, p. 139). They can question who is producing these images and why. Then, they can write against the mainstream images and depictions. Not only should teachers bring a critical media literacy lens into their classroom, but they should allow the students to write against the dominant narrative in creative ways via essays, narratives, and editorials (Muhammad & McArthur, 2015).

Performance Poetry

Performance poetry, or spoken word, was the second most common type of project. It is also sometimes called slam poetry, although as the name suggests, that refers to poetry that is performed at a poetry slam competition. Regardless of the term that is used, this type of poetry is written to be performed. Additionally, these poems often center around social justice topics such as inequality, racism, and poverty. Performance poetry can be used to validate students' language, culture, and identity, to develop literacy skills, and to enhance understandings of local activism (Ramirez & Jimenez-Silva, 2015). Highlighted below are an after school performance poetry project with Latino students in a southern California border town and one from a high school ELA classroom in Los Angeles.

Poetry on the Border. Although spoken word is typically associated with African American culture, it has a rich history in Latino culture in southern California (Ramirez & Jimenez-Silva, 2015). An example of how this can be used with Latino students is provided by Ramirez and Jimenez-Silva (2015), who held an after school and weekend performance poetry project in a city on the U.S./Mexico border. Due to the combination of standardized teaching, lack of student voice, and the students not being represented in the curriculum, this project was done after school and on Saturdays.

The project commenced with students reading multicultural poetry that was relevant to them. Ramirez and Jimenez-Silva (2015) "strongly recommend using a range of multicultural poetry, including Angelou (2000), 'I Know Why The Caged Bird Sings,' to engage students in discussing and examining issues concerning identity, schooling, and cultural backgrounds"(p. 89). They also recommend critically analyzing the poems, examining style and use of figurative language as well as themes, and having dialogue that links the students' experiences to the content of the poems. They found that "Latino youth were able to develop analytical skills reflective of extraordinary readers through poetry. The rich discussions students had about issues concerning equality and social justice informed and advanced their interpretive skills while examining diverse poetry" (Ramirez & Jimenez-Silva, 2015, p. 90).

The next step involved the instructor modeling a poem that he had written and then inviting poets from the community into the classroom. The instructors felt like it was critical to learn from members of the community who share common interests and a passion for writing and to emphasize the importance of literacy in community activism (Ramirez & Jimenez-Silva, 2015). The students then workshopped their own performance poetry (with topics of equality and social justice) utilizing peer feedback and performed their final pieces in front of their families and peers at a popular local park. "Students felt very proud about their poems and consequently, presented ideas and solutions they had for the community. For many, it was their first opportunity to share their view of transformation for their community" (Ramirez & Jimenez-Silva, 2015, p. 91). Not only were the students able to develop and use their voice, but they increased their literacy skills in the process.

Poetry in a Language Arts Classroom

In this example, Carmagian (2008) was a teacher who used social justice performance poetry in his 12th grade ELA classroom as part of his composition curriculum. The majority of his students were African American and 14% were Latino. The school was situated in a community that was known for gangs, violence, and racial conflict. Carmagian (2008) saw studying and performing political performance poetry as a way to move from competition amongst students to a shared "critical social analysis of power across socially constructed sets of differences" (p. 38). The end goal was for the students to "develop the type of critical social consciousness necessary for socially transformative action" (p. 40).

Carmagian (2008) drew from the Black Arts Movement in order to support his students' writing and performances of political poetry. He taught the history and the significance of movement and the role of spoken word poetry in the origins of rap music. That was a very popular music genre amongst his students so he was able to build upon that knowledge and promote engagement. Next, the students analyzed a film titled *Slam* (Lionsgate, 1998). With the film situated in its political and historical background, two essential questions were posed: "How does life in Dar City [the setting in *Slam*] compare and contrast to your lived experience? How did the characters in *Slam* use their words to change their world and what implications does this have on your duty as a poet?" (Carmagian, 2008, p. 42). The students then composed two spoken word pieces and performed them at a school assembly.

Multimodal Compositions

Multimodal compositions were the third most common type of written product. With the prevalence of technology, youth are consuming and composing texts in very different ways than in the past (Garcia et al., 2015). "The compositional practices of adolescents have undergone numerous shifts—from the page to the screen and from text to multimodal" (Smith, 2014, p. 1). In short, adolescents are increasingly using a variety of modes and media in their compositions. They may supplement the text they write with another mode (e.g. sound, video, drawings, images) or a combination of modes. Educators are now seeing value in multimodal literacies and are beginning to utilize multimodal compositions "for a variety of reasons—including to make schooling relevant, improve equity, prepare students to be critical and global citizens, and meet the needs of today's adolescents" (Smith, 2014, p. 2).

Multimodal compositions provide an engaging and beneficial medium for social justice projects. Highlighted below are two different youth research projects carried out by high school students. The first comes from an ethnographic research class where the students produced multimodal blogs and films. The other is from a participatory research project where the students create multimedia presentations of their findings.

Auto-Ethnographic Blogs and Films. This project was carried out in a small, public high school in New York City where the teacher taught a qualitative research course (DeJaynes, 2015). The students were trained as auto-ethnographers and investigated their experiences, beliefs, and cultures in order to build community and validate their identities. This process involved taking photos, recording and telling stories, and writing blogs and poetry. The students read and analyzed a poem titled "Where I'm From" (Lyon, n.d.). before writing their own "Where I'm From" poems. Language was considered to be one of the modes and the students were allowed to draw from their full range of linguistic resources (Farsi, Spanish, Creole, Russian, Korean, and other first languages were represented). "As youth interrogated into and crafted artful digital films to represent pieces of their identities, their stories, affiliations, personal and collective histories became textured sites of inquiry in our vibrant classroom community" (DeJaynes, 2015, p. 186).

For the blogs, the students were "asked to carefully curate five artifacts representing personal, social, and cultural affiliations" (DeJaynes, 2015, p. 191). One student chose a Yiddish folk song to represent her grandmother fleeing the Holocaust. Others selected artifacts such as family recipes and photographs. Not only did the students publish their blogs, but they shared their artifacts and the stories behind them with their classmates. The final product was an identity film in which the students had to present their artifacts and research. In order to prepare for that, DeJaynes (2015) and her co-teacher "modeled vulnerability and the possibility of keeping stories to yourself that you didn't want to share, whatever the reason. Representational choices were just that—choices" (p. 194).

The multimodal identity films were presented in a series of classroom film festivals. "The youth began with their own stories, pushing back against stereotypes or incomplete visions others held about them—and those they held about others. Many youth reflected on their surprise at the difference between how their peers typically author themselves at school and how they authored themselves their films" (DeJaynes, 2015, p. 195). Not only did this project help negotiate and affirm identities, but it helped humanize others and deepened understandings and personal connections. Students also honed both traditional and mulitimodal literacy skills.

Multimedia Research Presentations. The Council of Youth Research is comprised of professors and graduate students and teachers and students from select Los Angeles public high schools (Garcia et al., 2015). The students are African American and Latino and come from communities known for poverty and failing schools but also for resistance (e.g., South Central Los Angeles, East Los Angeles, Watts). Students who are interested in social justice are recommended by their teachers. Although the students attend a summer program, the teachers work with them throughout the school year in order to facilitate the development of their literacy skills and to help them prepare for their presentations. The teachers also work with the professors and graduate students to train the students in research methods and social theory to help them identify their research question. Then, the students gather data to answer those questions. "They develop surveys that they distribute to students both physically and online; they interview students, teachers, and community members; they observe schools and neighborhoods; and they analyze national data sets" (Garcia et al., 2015, p. 157). The students receive further guidance as they analyze the data and prepare multimedia presentations (e.g. PowerPoint and video) on their findings.

The students' audience ranges from other students to policymakers and politicians. They write reflections and keep the dialogue going via a website afterwards (Garcia et al., 2015). This project was intentionally designed to have the students utilize college-level reading, writing, and speaking practices, but also to have them become the experts and to draw from their funds of knowledge. "The Council situates literacy and learning as practices rooted in the lived experiences of its students and oriented toward action for personal empowerment and social justice" (Garcia et al., 2015, p. 162).

EXPANDING LITERACY PRACTICES: CLASSROOM STRATEGIES

The strategies listed below were utilized in many of the aforementioned social justice writing projects. They can be implemented in any classroom utilizing any curriculum.

Strategy 1: Translanguaging for Full Participation

One of the main strategies that can be used throughout various writing projects is translanguaging, or use of the students' full linguistic repertoires. Canagarajah (2011) defines it as "the ability of multilingual speakers to shuttle between languages, treating the diverse languages that form their repertoire as an integrated system" (p. 401). Students should not be limited to using English only, but rather, should be allowed to use their home languages in the classroom. Teachers can encourage students to do this not only during pre-writing and writing, but also as they are learning new content and skills. It is not necessary to know the students home language(s) to allow for translanguaging.

Strategy 2: Multimodal Expression for Integration of Various Modes and Media

Multimodal expressions through the use of multimodal compositions provide students ways to use technology as well as a variety of modes and media in writing. Teachers should use multimodal literacies as a form of addressing social justice, as these new literacies provide equitable opportunities for students to express themselves in engaging and valuable forms. The projects described in this chapter can be examples for teachers to modify and implement in their own classrooms.

IMPLICATIONS FOR LITERACY TEACHER EDUCATION

The recent NCTE (2012) social justice standard for initial teacher preparation (Standard VI) and the elements underneath it demonstrate the importance of teachers being able to use social justice practices in ELA classrooms:

> Element 1: Candidates plan and implement English language arts and literacy instruction that promotes social justice and critical engagement with complex issues related to maintaining a diverse, inclusive, equitable society. Element 2: Candidates use knowledge of theories and research to plan instruction responsive to students' local, national and international histories, individual identities (e.g., race, ethnicity, gender expression, age, appearance, ability, spiritual belief, sexual orientation, socioeconomic status, and community environment), and languages/dialects as they affect students' opportunities to learn in ELA. (NCTE, 2012, p. 1).

As the findings from the literature review and the highlighted projects show, writing for social justice provides an effective way to address this standard and its elements. It also shows a lot of promise both inside and outside of ELA classrooms. It can be adapted to fit into the curriculum or can be used in out of school settings. The reported outcomes of the projects are especially beneficial to CLD adolescents: increased social consciousness, increased critical literacy skills, developed voice, negotiated identities, and the ability to produce counternarratives. However, preparing teachers to effectively use social justice methods with CLD adolescents requires some programmatic planning.

First, teachers must be able to create a safe learning community in order to utilize social justice practices in their classrooms. It is imperative to provide voice and legitimacy to students with diverse perspectives and backgrounds (Glazier & Seo, 2005), and this requires a sense of safety. To establish this and to make the classroom student-centered, teachers must learn about their students' lives, the communities they live in, and their histories. In short, they need to learn about their students' funds of knowledge in order to successfully leverage them. The incorporation of González, Moll, and Amanti's (2005) text on this subject would greatly benefit teacher preparation programs.

Second, teachers must realize the structural issues (e.g. structural racism, structural poverty) and their histories that are the root cause of so many inequities that CLD students face in order to use a critical lens. After all, "racism is above everything, about practices and behaviors that produce a racial structure—a network of social relations at social, political, economic, and ideological levels that shapes the life chances of the various races" (Bonilla-Silva, 2015, p. 1360). These structures work together to perpetuate the "achievement gap," although Gloria Ladson-Billings (2006) says that we should call it an "education debt." That term implies the debt that we have to pay to compensate for a long and complicated history of inequitable and unjust treatment of CLD students in the United States. Social justice education provides one way of making payment on that debt, but the underlying causes of that debt must be fully understood.

Third, teachers must know and understand how to apply the theories behind social justice education. The two predominant ones from the literature review would create a solid foundation: critical literacy (Freire, 1970) and culturally relevant pedagogy (Ladson-Billings, 1995). Other multiculturalists (e.g. James Banks, Geneva Gay, Carol Lee, Sonia Nieto, Lisa Delpit, Christine Sleeter, Django Paris) have since contributed to this work and there is now a large body of literature to draw from, especially in the field of multicultural education. I believe that critical multicultural education should be a component of any teacher preparation program, if not a foundational course.

Finally, as teachers and teacher educators, we must examine our own positionality, or how our values, race, gender, religion, dis/ability, social class, and other aspects of our identity shape our understanding of the world. Not only is this necessary to facilitate discussions about difficult or controversial topics, but it is necessary to contemplate as students negotiate their own identity and positionality.

REFLECTION QUESTIONS

1. There are many different definitions of social justice. What does it mean to you and how might you utilize it?
2. What are the social justice issues in your school and/or your community? Who is doing social justice work there? How might these issues and resources be incorporated in your classroom?
3. How can you learn more about your students, their communities, assets, barriers, social justice interests, and funds of knowledge? And, how can you draw from this?
4. What do you need to learn more about in order to implement social justice education and/or writing for social justice?

REFERENCES

Alsup, J., & Miller, S. (2014). Reclaiming English education: Rooting social justice in dispositions. *English Education, 46*(3), 195–215.

Angelou, M. (2000). *I know why the caged bird sings.* New York, NY: Ballantine Books.

Bonilla-Silva, E. (2015). The structure of racism in color-blind, "post-racial" America. *American Behavioral Scientist, 59*(11), 1358–1376. doi: 10.1177/0002764215586826

Camangian, P. (2008). Untempered tongues: Teaching performance poetry for social justice. *English Teaching: Practice And Critique, 7*(2), 35–55.

Canagarajah, A. S. (2011). Codemeshing in academic writing: Identifying teachable strategies of translanguaging. *Modern Language Journal 95*(3), 401–417.

Chapman, T. K., Hobbel, N., & Alvarado, N. V. (2011). A social justice approach as a base for teaching writing. *Journal of Adolescent & Adult Literacy, 54*(7), 539–541. doi:1 0.1 598/JAAL.54.7.8

Coffey, H. (2011). *Critical literacy.* Retrieved June 10, 2016 from http://www.learnnc.org/lp/pages/4437?ref=search.

DeJaynes, T. (2015). "Where I'm from" and belonging: A multimodal, cosmopolitan perspective on arts and inquiry. *E-Learning and Digital Media 12*(2), 183–198. doi: 10.1177/2042753014567236

Freire, P. (1970). *Pedagogy of the oppressed* [Pedagogía del oprimido] (M. B. Ramos, Trans.). New York, NY: Seabury Press.

Garcia, A., & Gaddes, A. (2012). Weaving language and culture: Latina adolescent writers in an after-school writing project. *Reading & Writing Quarterly, 28*(2), 143–163. doi: 10.1080/10573569.2012.651076

Garcia, A., Mirra, N., Morrell, E., Martinez, A., & Scorza, D. (2015) The council of youth research: Critical literacy and civic agency in the digital age. *Reading & Writing Quarterly, 31*(2), 151–167. doi: 10.1080/10573569.2014.962203

Gee, J. P. (2000). Identity as an analytic lens for research in education. *Review of Research in Education, 25*, 99–125. doi: 10.2307/1167322

Glazier, J., & Seo, J.-A. (2005). Multicultural literature and discussion as mirror and window? *Journal of Adolescent & Adult Literacy, 48*(8), 686–700. https://doi.org/10.1598/JAAL.48.8.6

González, N., Moll, L. C., & Amanti, C. (2005). *Funds of knowledge: Theorizing practices in households, communities and classrooms.* Mahwah, NJ: Erlbaum.

Jocson, K. M. (2009). Steering legacies: Pedagogy, literacy, and social justice in schools. *Urban Review: Issues And Ideas In Public Education, 41*(3), 269–285. doi: 10.1007/s11256-008-0103-0

Ladson-Billings, G. (2006). From the achievement gap to the education debt: Understanding achievement in U.S. Schools. *Educational Researcher, 35*(7), 3–12.

Ladson-Billings, G. (1995). Toward a theory of culturally relevant pedagogy. *American Educational Research Journal, 32*(3), 465–491.

Ladson-Billings, G. (2006). From the achievement gap to education debt: Understanding achievement in U.S. schools. *Educational Researcher, 35*(7), 3–12.

Lionsgate Films (Producer). (1998). *Slam.* [DVD]. Available from http://www.lionsgate-shop.com

Lyon G.E. (n.d.) *Where I'm from.* Retrieved from http://www.georgeellalyon.com/where.html

Lopez, A. E. (2011). Culturally relevant pedagogy and critical literacy in diverse English classrooms: A case study of a secondary English teacher's activism and agency. *English Teaching, 10*(4), 75–93.

Mariconda, B. (2015, March 25). *Teaching voice in writing* [Web log comment]. Retrieved from https://empoweringwriters.com/teaching-voice-in-writing-barbara-mariconda/

McCarther, S. M., & Davis, D. M. (2015). Bravest girl in the world: Exploring social justice through adolescents' lens. *Journal of Urban Learning, Teaching, and Research, 11,* 50–56.

Miller, M. E. (2014). The power of conversation: Linking discussion of social justice to literacy standards. *Voices from the Middle, 22*(1), 36–42.

Muhammad, G. E., & McArthur, S. A. (2015). "Styled by their perceptions": Black adolescent girls interpret representations of black females in popular culture. *Multicultural Perspectives, 17*(3), 133–140. doi: 10.1080/15210960.2015.1048340

National Council for Teachers of English. (2012). NCTE/NCATE *standards for initial preparation of teachers of secondary English language arts, grades 7–12.* Retrieved from http://www.ncte.org/library/NCTEFiles/Groups/CEE/NCATE/ApprovedStandards_111212. pdf

Nieto, S., & Bode, P. (2008). *Affirming diversity: The sociopolitical context of multicultural education* (5th ed.). Boston, MA: Allyn and Bacon.

O'Brien, T. (1990). *The things they carried.* New York, NY: Houghton Mifflin.

Otheguy, R., García, O., & Reid, W. (2015). Clarifying translanguaging and deconstructing named languages: A perspective from linguistics. *Applied Linguistics Review, 6*(3), 281–307. doi: 10.1515/applirev-2015-0014

Ramirez, P. C., & Jimenez-Silva, M. (2015). The intersectionality of culturally responsive teaching and performance poetry: Validating secondary Latino youth and their community. *Multicultural Perspectives, 17*(2), 87–92. doi: 10.1080/15210960.2015.1022448

Scarbrough, B., & Allen, A. (2014). Writing workshop revisited: Confronting communicative dilemmas through spoken word poetry in a high school English classroom. *Journal of Literacy Research, 46*(4), 475–505. doi: 10.1177/1086296X15568929

Seher, R. (2011). Forging democratic spaces: Teachers and students transforming urban public schools from the inside. *Schools: Studies in Education, 8*(1), 166–189. doi: 10.1086/659445

Singer, J., & Shagoury, R. (2005). Stirring up justice: Adolescents reading, writing, and changing the world. *Journal of Adolescent & Adult Literacy, 49*(4), 318–339. doi: 10.1598/JAAL.49.4.5

Smith, B.E. (2014). Beyond words: A review of research on adolescents and multimodal composition. In R. E. Ferdig & K. E. Pytash (Eds.), *Exploring multimodal composition and digital writing* (pp. 1–19). Hershey, PA: IGI Global.

Stewart, M. A. (2015). My journey of hope and peace: Learning from adolescent refugees' lived experiences. *Journal of Adolescent & Adult Literacy, 59*(2), 149–159.

Tatum, A., & Gue, V. (2012). The sociocultural benefits of writing for African American adolescent males. *Reading & Writing Quarterly, 28*(2), 123–142. doi: 10.1080/10573569.2012.651075

Wissman, K.K. (2011). "Rise up!": Literacies, lived experiences, and identities within an in-school "other space." *Research in the Teaching of English, 45*(4), 405–438.

CONTRIBUTOR BIOGRAPHIES

EDITORS

Luciana C. de Oliveira, Ph.D., is Professor and Chair in the Department of Teaching and Learning in the School of Education and Human Development at the University of Miami, Florida. Her research focuses on issues related to teaching English language learners (ELLs) at the K–12 level, including the role of language in learning the content areas and teacher education, advocacy and social justice. She is the author or editor of 21 books and over 180 publications in various outlets. She is also the series editor of the University of Miami School of Education and Human Development Series with Information Age Publishing. She is President (2018–2019) of TESOL International Association.

Blaine E. Smith, Ph.D., is an Assistant Professor of New Literacies and Bi/Multilingual Immigrant Learners in the Department of Teaching, Learning & Sociocultural Studies at the University of Arizona. Her research focuses on the digital literacies of culturally and linguistically diverse adolescents across contexts, with special attention to their multimodal composing processes. Blaine's research has appeared in *Computers & Education, Journal of Second Language Writing, Written Communication, Bilingual Research Journal,* and *British Journal of Educa-*

Expanding Literacy Practices Across Multiple Modes and Languages for Multilingual Students, pages 113–116.
Copyright © 2019 by Information Age Publishing
All rights of reproduction in any form reserved.

tional Technology, among others. She is a 2016 National Academy of Education/ Spencer Postdoctoral Fellow.

AUTHORS

Mary A. Avalos is a Research Associate Professor in the Department of Teaching and Learning. Her research interests include bilingualism, second language, and multilingual teaching and learning in public schools, and using Systemic Functional Linguistics as a tool for language teaching. Most recently, she has worked with teachers to develop interventions that provide explicit instruction for academic language, or the language of schooling, in content areas, including reading/ language arts, mathematics, and social studies. She has directed funded projects for research and teacher development, and published her work in the *Bilingual Research Journal, Elementary School Journal*, and *The Reading Teacher.*

Daryl Axelrod is a doctoral student in Language and Literacy Learning in Multilingual Settings in the Department of Teaching and Learning at the University of Miami. His research interests focus on digital literacies and instructional technology use in culturally and linguistically diverse classroom settings.

Alain Bengochea, Ph.D., is an Assistant Professor in the Department of Educational and Clinical Studies at University of Nevada, Las Vegas. His research focuses on exploring the ideologies shaping emergent bilinguals' learning experiences in early and middle childhood settings and examining the multimodal resources (including translanguaging) available to and used by these learners. His research includes studying the multimodal choices of emergent bilinguals during naturally occurring interactions, such as in sociodramatic play; investigating the role of instructional practices in teacher-directed activities, such as in shared readings; and researching teachers' articulated and enacted beliefs and practices in English-medium and dual language settings.

Loren Jones, Ph.D., is a Clinical Assistant Professor and TESOL Program Coordinator at the University of Maryland, College Park. She recently completed her Ph.D. specializing in literacy and language learning for emergent bilingual students in the Department of Teaching and Learning at the University of Miami. She holds a Master's degree in Education with a specialization in Foreign Language Education. She has seven years' experience teaching Spanish at the secondary level in both traditional and online formats and is bilingual in English and Spanish. Her research focuses on best practices for literacy and language instruction to support English language learners and bilingual learners in the primary school context.

Kristin Kibler is a doctoral candidate in the Language and Literacy Learning in Multilingual Settings program at the University of Miami. She holds a Master's degree in Learning, Teaching, and Curriculum with an emphasis in TESOL. She has ten years of experience as a teacher and literacy coach, primarily within three urban school districts in the United States. Interests include improving educational outcomes for culturally and linguistically diverse adolescents through the use of social justice education, culturally relevant texts and pedagogy, critical literacy, newcomers programs, and bilingual education.

Irina Malova is an Assistant Professor of English in the Department of General Education at Miami Regional University. Her research focuses on literacy instruction for Emergent Bilinguals (EBs) and literacy development among EBs, in particular, integrated reading-writing instruction in elementary school.

Susan R. Massey is presently an Associate Professor at St. Thomas University where she has been a faculty member for the past nine years. She is director of the reading department in the Department of Education. Her research interests are in reading fluency and vocabulary for native and nonnative English speakers.

J. Andrés Ramírez is an Assistant Professor of TESOL and Bilingual Education in the Department of Curriculum, Culture, and Educational Inquiry at Florida Atlantic University. His research explores economic, cultural, and linguistic issues constraining and enabling the academic literacy achievement of culturally and linguistically diverse students in the US and on connecting these issues to advocacy and sound curricular practice. He anchors his academic work on poststructural materialism, critical discourse studies, critical pedagogy, and systemic functional linguistics (SFL).

Carolina Rossato de Almeida recently completed her Ph.D. specializing in Language and Literacy Learning in Multilingual Settings in the Department of Teaching and Learning at the University of Miami, Florida. She holds a Master's degree in Communication Studies with a specialization in Intercultural Communication. Her research investigates the interplay of translanguaging and multimodality in polycultural picture books.

Sabrina F. Sembiante is an Assistant Professor of TESOL and Bilingual Education in the Department of Curriculum, Culture, and Educational Inquiry at Florida Atlantic University. Her research agenda comprises two interconnected themes: The first is to investigate instructional practices that support emergent bilingual students' developing bilingualism, biliteracy, and academic language in school contexts. The second is to promote and advocate for multilingualism as a human right in education and to seek justice for multilingual and multidialectal teacher and student populations in the U.S. She frames her research from sociocultural and systemic functional linguistic perspectives. Her research has been published in Language and Education, Bilingual Research Journal, Journal of Early Childhood Literacy, and Curriculum Inquiry.

Sharon L. Smith is a doctoral student specializing in literacy and language learning for multilingual students in the Department of Teaching and Learning at the University of Miami. She holds Bachelor's degrees in Elementary Education and Spanish with a specialization in Reading Instruction. After completing a Fulbright ETA Grant in Colombia, she taught elementary school for two years before pursuing her Ph.D. Her research interests focus on best practices for multimodal literacy and language instruction to support emerging bilingual learners at the elementary level.

Made in the USA
Middletown, DE
16 January 2024

47976482R00071